Beautiful Easy Flower Gardens

*Step-by-Step and Seasonal Plans
for a Colorful, Exciting Landscape*

Laurence Sombke

Rodale Press, Emmaus, Pennsylvania

OUR MISSION

We publish books that empower people's lives.

RODALE BOOKS

The information in this book has been carefully researched, and all efforts have been made to ensure accuracy. Rodale Press, Inc., assumes no responsibility for any injuries suffered or damages or losses incurred during the use of or as a result of following this information. It is important to study all directions carefully before taking any action based on the information and advice presented in this book. When using any commercial product, always read and follow label directions. Where trade names are used, no discrimination is intended and no endorsement by Rodale Press, Inc., is implied.

On the cover: Cosmos, gloriosa daisies, and yarrow are just a few of the spectacular but easy-to-grow annuals and perennials featured in this book.

If you have any questions or comments concerning this book, please write to:

Rodale Press, Inc.
Book Readers' Service
33 East Minor Street
Emmaus, PA 18098

Beautiful Easy Flower Gardens Editorial and Design Staff
Managing Editor: Ellen Phillips
Editor: Barbara W. Ellis
Garden Designer: Laurence Sombke
Cover and Interior Book Designer: Darlene Schneck
Interior Illustrators: Frank Fretz and Elayne Sears
Interior Layout: Deborah Kriger and Richard Snyder
Photography Layout: Diane Ness Shaw
Photography Research: Heidi A. Stonehill
Copy Editor: Nancy N. Bailey
Editorial Assistance: Nancy Kutches
Manufacturing Coordinator: Patrick T. Smith
Indexer: Nan N. Badgett

Rodale Books
Vice President, Editorial Director, Home and Garden:
    Margaret Lydic Balitas
Art Director, Home and Garden: Michael Mandarano
Copy Director, Home and Garden: Dolores Plikaitis
Office Manager, Home and Garden: Karen Earl-Braymer
Editor-in-Chief: William Gottlieb

Library of Congress Cataloging-in-Publication Data

Sombke, Laurence.
    Beautiful easy flower gardens : step-by-step and seasonal plans for a colorful, exciting landscape / by Laurence Sombke.
        p.   cm.
    Includes bibliographical references (p.) and index.
    ISBN 0–87596–700–0 (hc : alk. paper).
    1. Flower gardening. 2. Low maintenance gardening. 3. Gardens—Design. I. Title.
    SB405.S665 1995
    635.9—dc20   95–30544

Distributed in the book trade by St. Martin's Press

2 4 6 8 10 9 7 5 3 1   hardcover

I dedicate this book to the listeners
of my radio program, "The Natural Gardener,"
on Northeast Public Radio, the readers of my newspaper
and magazine columns, the people who come
to my lectures and seminars, the people who
have asked me to design their gardens and landscapes,
and all of the people who have helped me
along the way.

I also dedicate this book to Tim Steinhoff, the horticulturist
at Montgomery Place in
Annandale-on-Hudson, New York, and Joel Allen,
the horticulturist at Cornell Cooperative
Extension of Columbia County in Hudson, New York,
for tirelessly and cheerfully answering
all of my gardening questions.

*F*inally, I dedicate this book to my wife,
Catherine Herman, who is always coming up
with new garden experiments that I
would never think about.

Contents

PART TWO
DESIGNS FOR BEAUTIFUL EASY GARDENS

Welcome to Beautiful Easy Gardening

THE NATIONAL GARDENING ASSOCIATION tells us that gardening is the number-one leisure-time activity in the United States. I don't doubt it, but who has leisure time anymore? Like most of you, I have a family that needs my attention, a house that needs maintenance, and a career to pursue. I have a radio show to produce, books and magazine articles to write, the garbage to take out, and a million other things to do. My son wants to go to baseball practice, and my daughter wants me to read her a book.

Even with all that, I can't imagine giving up my flower gardens. Instead, I have developed a low-maintenance approach to gardening that allows me to have my garden and my family life, too. That doesn't mean my garden looks wretched, unkept, or messy. It also doesn't mean I only grow the common, ordinary annuals found in every garden center and grocery store in spring. I want a garden that is more interesting than that!

In this book, I've shared all my secrets of growing a garden that looks beautiful for months and yet is easy to maintain. Part 1, "Making a Beautiful Easy Garden," covers everything you need to know to plan, plant, and care for a beautiful easy garden.

Part 2, "Designs for Beautiful Easy Gardens," features designs for 11 beautiful easy gardens for you to plant and grow. Each comes with descriptions of the plants, tips on the best cultivars to look for, and step-by-step directions that take you through your first year of planting and caring for your garden.

Throughout the book, you'll find special photo galleries that show beautiful easy flower gardens and colorful combinations. They'll give you plenty of inspiration to transform your own garden—or your whole yard!—into the kind of show you used to only dream about. It's easy!

Making a Beautiful Easy Garden

It's easy to have a beautiful
flower garden. Just follow the
simple steps in this section
and your garden can't fail.

CHAPTER ONE

Beautiful Easy Basics

How to Have a Beautiful Easy Garden

I LOVE TO GARDEN. Digging in the soil is relaxing for me. It's good exercise, too. I also love discovering and planting plants that I have never grown before and enjoying all the beauty that a flower garden adds to my yard. Over the years, I have looked for ways to have beautiful gardens that are easy to maintain. I've found that there are hundreds of annuals, perennials, bulbs, roses, flowering shrubs, and vines that are easy to grow and look beautiful. Those plants play a central role in my beautiful easy gardens. But picking out a bunch of plants at a garden center doesn't necessarily create a garden — and it certainly doesn't make it beautiful *and* easy.

I've found that the best gardens start out with a concept or theme. You can see what I mean if you page through the garden designs included in Part 2. You'll find a garden for hot, dry soil, another for a boggy site, one for attracting butterflies, and yet another for planting along a picket fence (plus 7 more!). All of them are filled with great-looking, easy-to-grow plants, combined to give you months of pleasure.

But that isn't the end of the story. I can all but guarantee that you'll be growing great flower gardens next season if you remember the following four principles:

1. Keep your garden small.
2. Let your yard help pick your garden.
3. Stop using chemicals.
4. Don't treat your soil like dirt.

KEEP YOUR GARDEN SMALL

IT IS LOTS less frustrating to grow a few things well than a lot of things poorly. The gardens in this book are small enough that you can easily prepare the soil over the course of a weekend and plant one in an hour or two. As your confidence grows and you discover new plants that would look nice in your garden, you can always make it larger. You can also plant more of the gardens in this book in some other parts of your yard once you have the first one established and growing strongly.

Although preparing the soil and planting take a bit of a time investment, none of these gardens is very difficult or time-consuming to care for. That's especially true since you will be building better soil every year. And the better your soil, the easier it is to garden.

LET YOUR YARD HELP PICK YOUR GARDEN

ONE WAY to create a garden that is easy to care for is to choose flowers that would be happy in your yard the way it is. That doesn't mean you'll be growing a garden full of weeds! What it does mean is that you'll let the soil,

exposure, and other conditions in your yard help you decide what to grow. (But don't give up if your heart is set on growing a certain kind of plant like roses and your site seems more suited to growing drought-tolerant cacti. If you concentrate on improving your soil, you can turn it into a happy home for roses.)

To let your yard help pick your garden, start by reading Chapter 2. As you fill out your site survey, look for clues that will help you identify what plants will grow best. Sometimes, it's just a matter of taking your time and watching to see what's growing there already. I moved into an old colonial house and inherited the garden of a 96-year-old woman. She had planted little bits of this and that here and there. If I had been in a hurry to till under her beds or yank out every little bit of greenery I didn't recognize, I would have destroyed the fabulous forget-me-nots, evening primroses, squills, and other shade-loving plants I still don't know the names of.

So spend some time getting to know your landscape, especially if you have a new one to take care of that you haven't experienced for an entire blooming season. There may be some wonderful jewels growing there that you will destroy if you are too eager to make changes.

You may be surprised by what's struggling to survive in those corners of your yard that you mow just to keep the "weeds" chopped back. When I stopped mowing a narrow strip of weedy lawn on the north side of my house, I discovered a wonderful bed of fall-blooming New York asters.

If you have overgrown beds with flowers mixed in with weeds, use the designs in this book to help you pick flowers to grow with what's already there. Watch to see which plants are growing best, and add new plants from the designs in Part 2 to replace the weaker plants and weeds. (Take leaves and flowers of plants that you don't recognize to your local garden center to have them identified.)

Another way to make your garden more carefree is to grow plants that well-stocked local garden centers and nurseries offer. Most are in the business of pleasing their cus-tomers, and that means selling plants that will grow well in your area. They know from experience what works and what doesn't. Be wary of large-scale chain stores. More often than not, they don't have experts on staff, and the plants they offer are ordered regionally or nationally.

Another good source of plants that will grow well in your area is plant sales and swaps sponsored by local garden clubs and public gardens. Generally, these plants have been dug up that very day and are offered because they grow so well that the gardener who brought them has extras to spare.

STOP USING CHEMICALS

MOST PEOPLE who hear me on the radio, read my books, or come to my seminars want to work in a garden where they won't be exposed to harmful chemicals. The good news is you simply don't need all those expensive, potentially dangerous pesticides, fungicides, and fertilizers to have a beautiful garden. Some of the world's most famous and beautiful gardens were grown entirely without chemicals, and yours can be, too. Chemicals are a short-term solution to a long-term problem. But they cause many more problems than they solve. Chemical fertilizers drive away earthworms, kill beneficial insects and birds, seep into groundwater, and endanger children and pets playing on newly sprayed lawns.

Creating a healthy, environmentally friendly garden takes a little bit

A garden is a place to enjoy, where you can smell the fresh air and flowers and the kids can play. Why spoil the scene with chemicals?

more work up front but a lot less work down the road. Building rich soil, as you will learn to do in Chapter 4, builds success into your garden from the start. It lets you prevent problems rather than wait for them to occur. As a result, you won't need to spend time mixing and spraying chemicals that you would rather not use anyway.

By building rich soil and staying away from chemicals, you are going to create a fabulous flowering environment that encourages allies like beneficial insects, soil-building micro-organisms and earthworms, insect-eating toads, and more. Your garden will be a safe place for birds to visit and lunch on grubs, aphids, and other destructive insects. All of these creatures will help keep your garden in balance and prevent pests and dis-eases from getting out of control.

DON'T TREAT YOUR SOIL LIKE DIRT

AND THAT brings me to my last point. Too many people plant flowers, spray on fertilizer, and then wonder why their flowers look sickly and droop during the first sign of drought in sum-mer. The problem is that beautiful gar-dens need beautiful soil. And yes, soil *can* be beautiful. The moist, organically fertile soil you will learn to build will have a rich, earthy smell. It will be teeming with life — earthworms, soil microorganisms, and plant roots. And it will grow beautiful flowers —with very little help from you.

And now that I've delivered my sermon on what makes a beautiful easy garden, I can get down off my soapbox, put on my gardening shoes, and head for the garden. Care to join me?

Planning Your Garden

Finding the Flower Garden That's Best for You

As a GARDEN DESIGNER, I'm contacted spring, summer, and fall by home-owners asking for help with their landscapes. These would-be gardeners want everything from help designing a single flower bed to a plan for their entire landscape. Generally, they have an idea of what they want to plant. They come to me because they just aren't sure if they can do what they want given the kind of climate, soil, and sun they have on their property. In addition, they want to make sure they will have the time it takes to plant and care for a garden — and that a garden that's easy to care for won't be boring to look at.

You probably have similar dreams, ideas, and questions about your own landscape. (After all, if you didn't, you wouldn't be reading this book!) In this chapter, you'll learn how planning — and doing a little homework — is the secret to having a garden that's both beautiful and easy to take care of. But don't worry — the process I use is easy and fun. It's like being on a trea-sure hunt: The more clues you uncover, the closer you are to having the garden you've always dreamed of right in your own backyard.

During this garden treasure hunt, you'll be looking for clues as to what kind of garden you want and need and what conditions you'll be dealing with when you plant your first garden. Use the information you gather to decide where in your yard you would like to plant one of the flower gar-dens I've included in Part 2. As you answer the questions and complete the exercises in this chapter, you'll learn more about how to pick the best site and the perfect garden for you.

START WITH QUESTIONS

THE FIRST time I meet with a new client, they're nearly always full of questions about their landscape. They may start by asking me about particular plants they have growing in their yards. A typical question might be, "I have this barberry bush growing here, but it seems to be crowding this other bush. What should I do?" Or they want to know about planning and planting a special landscape feature they've always wanted. "I want a place where I can sit outside, read the paper, and enjoy nature. What should I plant and where should I plant it?"

That's when I start asking questions of my own so I can find out what kind of garden they would really like to have. As you start your own plan, I suggest you ask yourself—and other members of your family—some of the questions I ask my clients. Throughout this chapter, you'll find questions to ask yourself. (See "Getting Started" on this page for a list of questions to get started with.) You'll find that the answers you come up with will help you plan a garden or landscape that you and your family will *really* enjoy.

GETTING STARTED

HERE ARE SOME QUESTIONS that will help you start thinking about what kind of garden you would enjoy most. You'll enjoy the garden you create more if you think about these now.

• How much time per week do you want to devote to your garden?

• What kinds of flowers do you enjoy most?

• Do you want to grow flowers to cut for bouquets to bring indoors, or do you just want to make an attractive landscape around your home?

• Where would you enjoy viewing flowers most? Around your patio? From the living-room window? On either side of your doorstep?

• Are there places in your yard where you have always wanted to grow flowers?

• What activities do you like to do in your yard?

LEARN ABOUT YOUR SITE

AFTER I ask some basic questions, I take a long, slow walk around my client's yard. I carry a notebook and make a lot of notes about the conditions I observe: the amount of sunlight or shade the yard receives, the soil conditions, and so forth. I usually draw a map of the yard that indicates all the major features, including the house, garage, existing gardens, and major trees and shrubs.

This process, which is called making a site survey, is very important because it helps me learn all about the conditions I have to work with. I use the information I gather to select flowers and other plants that will thrive in the conditions that already exist on the site. I also use it to determine where flower gardens and other plantings will fit into the landscape.

You'll want to conduct your own site survey before you decide which

Start your garden plan by making a rough sketch of your yard in a garden notebook. Mark off the size of your yard and the flower gardens you have or want to plant in it. Draw in your house, trees, and other features. Don't worry about being artistic. Just make basic observations that will help you decide where to plant this year and in future seasons.

flower garden to plant and where to plant it. A site survey will provide you with all kinds of data that will help you make good decisions about which flower garden to plant and where it will thrive. There's simply no sense trying to plant a bright, sun-loving "El Diablo Drought-Tolerant Garden" (see page 219) if you have a yard full of dense shade. With lots of effort, you may get the plants to survive, but they won't thrive and bloom, and who wants to work hard for a garden full of sickly looking flowers? Instead, fill that shady site with flowers that love the shade—"A Shady Woodland Wildflower Garden" on page 133 is chock-full of them.

One cardinal rule of any site survey is *write it down*. If you don't keep notes in writing about all the questions you're answering and the observations you're making, time will pass and the next thing you know, you won't remember any of the details. To start your site survey, buy a notebook or diary and use it to keep all your notes about your garden. Now I know this isn't a life-and-death situation. If you don't write things down, you'll still probably be able to muddle through adding a flower garden this year.

When you want to tackle another garden goal next year or the year after, though, you'll have to start back at square one and do a new site survey.

SIZE UP YOUR PROPERTY

Even if you're just looking for that perfect site to plant one of the flower gardens I have included in this book, it pays to look at your entire yard and examine all the options. You're liable to miss some great opportunities—and create some headaches—if you just plop your garden down in the first spot that seems okay to you.

If you have a survey map of your property, you'll easily be able to tell its size and shape. If you don't have a survey map, measure your property with stakes and string or simply pace off the dimensions to get a general idea of its size and shape.

Draw a rough map of your yard in your notebook. (You can take notes directly on a copy of your survey, if you like, and keep it in your note-book.) Then measure your house, garage, and other buildings, and add them to your map. If you like, you can take the dimensions you've gathered and draw a scale map of your property to use for planning, but a rough map will be fine for any planning you're going to do now.

PICK SOME PRIME GARDEN SPOTS

SOMETIMES THE BEST PLACE to plant flowers is where they aren't expected. While you are doing your site survey, look for spots that you haven't ever considered planting with flowers. For example, what about planting a cheerful flower garden instead of foundation shrubs alongside your house? You'll find a design for just that in "Up Against a Wall" on page 233.

Did you know you can actually solve problems with flowers? Say good-bye to muddy spots you hate to mow with the garden in "Don't Get Bogged Down" on page 263. Or just plant a "Welcome Home" sign for yourself by lining your driveway with a classic perennial border—see "Beautiful Easy Perennials" on page 93.

IDENTIFY YOUR PRIME SPOTS

Within the large dimensions of your property, there are probably some smaller areas that you have already planned to turn into gardens of some type. Measure these areas and record them in your notebook, either right on your rough map or on a new rough drawing of part of your yard— of the back or side yard, for example.

But before you actually start planting those sites you've always assumed you'd plant, look around for a few new prime spots you haven't thought of before. See "Pick Some Prime Garden Spots" on this page for some ideas on what to look for.

GET TO KNOW YOUR TREES

One step in doing a site survey is to identify the trees you have growing on your property and make a note of their approximate sizes. Why? Because different trees have different characteristics that will affect the garden design that's right for you and your property. For example, oak trees are generally deep-rooted and have very strong wood. They are great shade trees, seldom lose branches in high winds, and create the perfect

spot for making a garden with wildflowers and shade-loving perennials.
Silver maples, on the other hand,
aren't such well-behaved landscape
specimens. Although they grow very
quickly, they are very weak-wooded
and often lose branches in high
winds. Worst of all for gardeners,
though, are their shallow roots, which
crowd out nearly any plant that at-
tempts to grow beneath them.

So take some time to get to know
your trees. The more you know about
them, the easier it will be to work
them into your overall landscape plan
and select flowers to grow under and
around them. Do you have oaks,
maples, lindens, or walnuts? Take a
look at your evergreens, too, and determine which types you have—
pines, spruces, cedars, or other
species. Use a tree identification guide
to help you. You'll find several listed
in "Recommended Reading" on page
277, or ask at your local library.

Learning the names of the trees
you have is just a small part of the
story. Try to find out as much as you
can about their growth habits. Are
your trees near their mature size? Are
they long- or short-lived? Do you
have species that are prone to problems? Here's where gardening books
on trees (as opposed to field guides

Callery pear

Pin oak

Sugar maple

Black walnut

Littleleaf linden

White pine

**The kinds of trees you have in your yard
often make a big difference in the type of
garden you can grow. Identifying your
trees will give you a head start on a beautiful easy garden.**

that will just help you identify them) are most valuable. Obviously, you can tell at a glance how tall your trees are, but find out how tall they are going to get, too. Is the pretty little 'Bradford' callery pear going to engulf your yard when it reaches its mature size of nearly 50 feet? Also look for information on problems that may crop up, such as a tendency to be weak-wooded. 'Bradford' pears, silver maples, and mulberries all share this characteristic. Use this information to help you decide which trees to take out, if any. And once you've figured out what kinds of trees are growing in your yard, you can read up on the care and pruning your trees need. You need to be extra vigilant about pruning weak-wooded trees, especially if they're planted right next to your house.

Don't just depend on book learning, though. You'll learn volumes by doing a little sleuthing yourself. With a garden shovel or fork, dig gently under your trees to determine if surface roots would make it difficult or impossible to plant under them. Do the trees have tiny leaves that seem to disappear as soon as they drop or large leaves that you have to rake off the garden? How much shade do they cast during the spring,

summer, and fall? For example, honey locusts cast very light dappled shade from spring to fall. Norway maples, on the other hand, cast such dense shade and have such shallow roots that it's hard to grow anything under them at all.

Can you tell what condition your trees are in? Are they old and in serious decline or badly in need of pruning? Should you consider replacing them altogether? Are there limbs that have been damaged by storms and may need to be removed? If you're unsure about any of these questions, look in your telephone book for a professional tree care company that employs arborists certified by the International Society of Arboriculture (ISA). They'll be able to help you evaluate your trees and plan how to care for them.

FUN IN THE SUN — OR MADE IN THE SHADE?

The kinds of flowers you'll be able to grow depend on the amount, duration, and time of day when the sun shines on your garden. In fact, sun and shade are probably the foremost factors in determining what kind of flower garden to grow. It's fairly easy to improve poor soil by adding organic matter, for example, but moving a garage or house to get more sun is a little bit more difficult!

You can always remove lower branches on tall trees to add a little sunlight to a yard, but that's generally just a temporary solution. Eventually, the tree's branches will grow and shade the site again, although you may be able to buy yourself a few years of sun in the process. Since removing limbs can be dangerous and can also damage the tree or destroy its shape, it's a good idea to call in an expert arborist to take care of the job for you.

To determine the amount of sun or shade your potential garden spot receives, draw a little picture of your yard in your notebook, and note north, south, east, and west. Then, throughout the day, watch the area you want to plant with flowers. Make a note when the sun begins to strike your potential garden site in the morning, and keep track of how long it shines directly on it. If it becomes shaded during part of the day, in late afternoon, for example, jot down when. If your site does get shade, make a note of which trees or buildings are casting the shade. If your yard is typical, you'll have sites with a combination of sun and shade, which will give you a lot of exciting flower

garden opportunities. Here's how to tell what kind of sun exposure your yard or garden is getting.

Full sun. You need to have at least six to eight hours of direct sun each day to grow flowers that are listed in books and catalogs as requiring full sun. You may find that your site receives either morning or afternoon sun only, but as long as the site receives six to eight hours of sun, you'll be fine with full-sun flowers. Sites on the east side of your house will receive morning sun; on the west side, afternoon sun. Sites that receive morning sun tend to be cooler than those that receive afternoon sun.

Partial sun or shade. Part sun and part shade are very similar. These mean your garden gets full sun for maybe two to three hours a day, followed by light shade for the rest of the day. They can also mean that your garden gets a good amount of sun, off and on each day, filtered through the branches of the trees overhead.

Shade. Your yard is shady if trees or buildings block most of the sunlight throughout the day. (A shady yard may receive a little sunshine off and on during the day.) The area right around the north side of your house will probably be in shade for most of the day. The south side of your house will get the most sun because the sun travels from east to west in the southern half of the sky. Don't be discouraged if you have a shady yard. Shade is good. It helps keep your house cool during the summer, and there are many wonderful shade-loving plants you can grow, from hostas and ferns to colorful wild-flowers.

One thing to keep in mind is that all shade isn't the same. Evergreens like pines cast dense shade all year round. It's very difficult to grow anything at all under them. Deciduous trees like oaks, which lose their leaves each fall, are another story altogether. They're a perfect place for growing spring bulbs like daffodils as well as many wildflowers that only require sun in the spring when they're growing and blooming. (You'll find a beautiful easy design for a shade-loving garden in Part 2 — see "A Shady Woodland Wildflower Garden" on page 133.)

RECORD YOUR TRAFFIC PATTERNS

You may think traffic is only for highways, but think again. Your garden plan should take into account how you use your yard, and that means accommodating traffic patterns. I'm not just talking about the cement walkway from your driveway to the front door here, although that certainly represents one type of traffic pattern. A practical plan also accommodates informal walkways. For example, is there a path you use between your house and garage or garbage cans? Or from your kitchen door out to the vegetable garden or compost pile? These are examples of informal walkways. In most cases, they are simply paths worn right in the lawn. Jot down the approximate locations of any walkways—formal or informal—on the property map you sketched in your notebook. That way you'll remember where they are and avoid planting over them when you plan where to put your new flower garden.

Be sure to jot down notes about how other members of your family like to use the yard. Does your spouse like to entertain in a shady corner of the lawn? Do the kids like to play soccer or baseball on the lawn? Do they have—or want—a playhouse out back? I've had to give up several garden ideas because it just isn't fair to tell the kids they can't play in the backyard. After all, it's their yard, too!

It's also a losing battle trying to grow flowers right next to a ball field, unless you're willing to police the area every minute of the day. And who wants to do that?

Don't think of traffic patterns as a problem: They actually give you planting opportunities. For example, planting a perennial border like the one in "Beautiful Easy Perennials" on page 93 right across the path to the garage is asking for trouble. Instead, look for ways you can spruce up a pathway, planting flowers so you can enjoy them as you walk along it.

Don't forget to make notes about how you like to relax in your yard, too. Perhaps you have—or would like to have—a quiet sitting area out back for reading and sipping iced tea on a hot summer day. If so, jot down a reminder in your notebook and perhaps circle an approximate location, so you will remember to surround it with flowers you'll enjoy. Or maybe you have a picnic table, either set up right by the kitchen door or out back in a shady spot where it's quiet and peaceful. Either way, you'll want to plan your garden so it's easy to carry picnic supplies back and forth from the kitchen. There's nothing worse than having to wind around obstacles when your hands are full!

LOOK FOR PLANTING OPPORTUNITIES

Every yard has problem spots that are difficult to manage. But whether you have a sunbaked site with hard-packed soil, where even weeds struggle to grow, or a steep slope that is a trial to mow, don't think of it as a problem. Instead, think of it as an opportunity. I like to look for ways to turn these types of sites into unique and beautiful parts of the backyard landscape. That's why so many of my garden designs in Part 2 can be used to transform problem sites into beautiful easy gardens.

So take a look around your yard and make notes about all the "opportunities" you see. Do you have a steep slope, rock wall, terraced retaining wall, or other obstructions to deal with? How about a foundation or shed you want to hide? Have you always wanted to do something about that uninviting, sunbaked slab of a patio that seems stuck out in the backyard surrounded by a sea of lawn? How about dressing it up with "Beautiful Easy Annuals" on page 107? If you have neighbors or a commercial property too close to your house, consider lining the edge of your property with the tall-growing plants in the "Up Against a Wall" garden on page 233. Do you have a pond or stream on your property that floods periodically? No problem! Turn to "Don't Get Bogged Down" on page 263 for options. Then keep these opportunities in mind when you design your flower garden.

What about garden features you've always wanted, like a cutting garden or a garden of old-fashioned flowers? Now's your chance to fulfill those dreams, too. (See "Beautiful

To turn a problem spot into a planting opportunity, just figure out what plants would be happy growing there. Lawn grass would languish in a wet site like this one, but hostas, ferns, and primroses thrive here. You'll find more ideas for a boggy site in "Don't Get Bogged Down" on page 263.

Easy Annuals" on page 107 and "Hollyhocks, Phlox, and Four-o'Clocks" on page 175.) If you simply love puttering and caring for unusual plants, perhaps you should find room for a rock garden like the one in "A Beautiful Easy Rock Garden" on page 249. Love roses but don't think you have the time for them? "Beautiful Easy Roses" on page 119 will help you fill your yard with beautiful, fragrant blooms without filling up your calendar with an endless schedule of sprays, dusts, and fertilizer applications.

WHAT'S YOUR CLIMATE?

BEFORE you can pick out plants that will thrive in your yard, you need to take time to consider the conditions they'll have to endure. One of the best ways to gauge your climate is to find out how cold it gets in winter, since many plants can only survive a certain amount of cold. Lucky for us, it's easy to figure out winter low temperatures by determining your area's plant hardiness zone. If you don't already know what hardiness zone you live in, start by finding where your garden is located on the map on page 20. This map, which was developed by the U.S. Department of Agriculture, shows 11

climate zones that are based on the average winter low temperature. Zone 1, which is coldest, is located in northern Alaska and Canada. In winter, Zone 1 temperatures can drop below minus 50°F! At the other extreme, gardens in Zone 11, located only in the Florida Keys, portions of southern California, and Hawaii, never get below a balmy 40°F in the winter.

Except for annuals, which live for only one growing season anyway, you really shouldn't try to grow plants that aren't fully hardy in your area. It's fine to experiment with a plant or two—perhaps ones that are hardy in Zone 6 if you live in Zone 5, for example. After all, you may find they're perfectly happy in your garden during even the worst of winters. But if you live in Zone 5 and you plant a whole garden of Zone 6 plants, you stand to lose them all during a colder-than-average winter.

Obviously, the average winter low temperature your garden receives is only a small part of the overall climate. The temperature, rainfall, and other conditions during the summer are just as important. As part of your site survey, make some notes about the growing conditions that are most important in your garden. Your observations will help you identify plants

USDA Plant Hardiness Zone Map

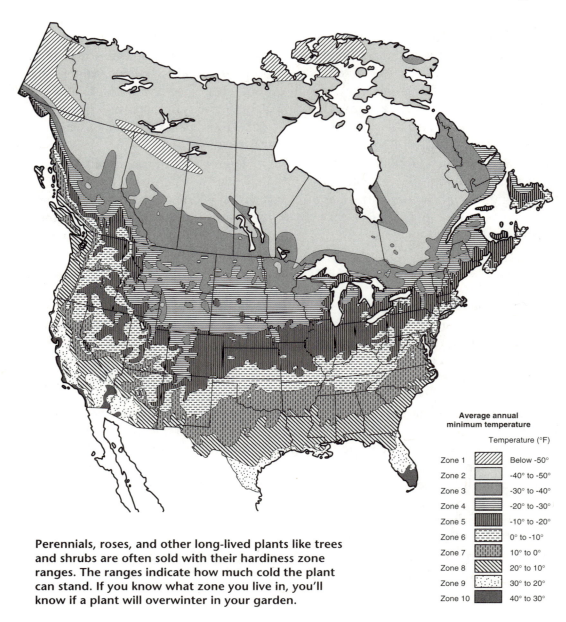

Average annual minimum temperature

Temperature (°F)

Zone 1	Below -50°
Zone 2	-40° to -50°
Zone 3	-30° to -40°
Zone 4	-20° to -30°
Zone 5	-10° to -20°
Zone 6	0° to -10°
Zone 7	10° to 0°
Zone 8	20° to 10°
Zone 9	30° to 20°
Zone 10	40° to 30°

Perennials, roses, and other long-lived plants like trees and shrubs are often sold with their hardiness zone ranges. The ranges indicate how much cold the plant can stand. If you know what zone you live in, you'll know if a plant will overwinter in your garden.

that will grow well in your garden. If you live in the Southeast, for example, you will want to plant flowers that can withstand the heat and humidity of your summer without complaint. In the West, summer drought will be an important factor.

If you're not sure what your biggest gardening challenges will be, ask the agents at your local Cooperative Extension Service office (listed under city or county governments in the telephone book) or the experts at a local garden center or nursery.

GET TO KNOW YOUR SOIL

LET ME start out by saying you can improve any soil, even the worst heavy clay or sandy soils. A lot of people have trouble gardening because they don't learn enough about their soil and don't really try to improve it. That's too bad, since improving soil is easy. You'll find complete information on learning more about your soil, improving it, preparing new garden beds, and dealing with problem soils in Chapter 4.

Getting to know your soil can help you plan a garden. Once you have read through Chapter 4, you will be able to tell whether you have

problem soil or average to good soil. (You may already know!) While you're looking through the designs in Part 2, look for plants that might be happy in the soil you already have. Plants that will grow in your existing soil will absolutely thrive in it once you've improved it. As a result, they will need much less help from you to grow and do well. For example, if you have dry, sandy soil, the plants in "An El Diablo Drought-Tolerant Garden" on page 219 might be good choices. The plants in the "Don't Get Bogged Down" garden on page 263, on the other hand, would mean a lot of extra work for you.

Another way to let your soil help you plan is to look for the sites with the best soil in your yard. Take a garden spade or fork out and dig a few test holes. (You can fill them right back up once you've had a chance to see what's underneath.) You'll find compacted soil on sites where cars are occasionally parked, and you may find building rubble near foundations. Those types of sites can still be made into beautiful gardens, but they will take more work than an abandoned vegetable garden or a weedy site along a fence. It's a good idea to write your observations in your notebook. Jot down notes about which sites seem most promising and which sites would take lots of work to improve.

CHOOSING THE GARDEN THAT'S RIGHT FOR YOU

CHOOSING the right flower garden to plant in your landscape is a very personal decision. Only you can decide what style of garden you like, what colors of flowers you want to plant, and how you would like to arrange them. The information you gather in a site survey will help you decide what to plant and where to plant it, but the style is up to you. That's why many of the designs in Part 2 leave the choice of flower colors up to you. Think of my designs as a jumping-off point and adapt them to your own yard and tastes. Choose flowers in a color scheme you enjoy, bend a border design in the middle to fit into a corner of your yard, or rearrange a rectangular design into a free-form amoeba-shaped one. The most important thing is to have fun with your garden.

Don't worry, though—help is at hand if you need some tips before making up your mind. There are some guiding principles that can help you get the right garden in the right place. Ask yourself the questions listed below. Then use your answers to help get you going in the right direction.

WHAT STYLE GARDEN DO YOU HAVE IN MIND?

You probably already have an idea of what kinds of gardens appeal to you. Do you like the look and feel of a tidy formal garden with everything planted in neat rows? Or do you prefer a more naturalistic garden with no straight lines and flowers growing in natural-looking drifts? Take the time to think about what type of garden styles appeal to you, and jot down some thoughts about them in your notebook. If you're not sure what you like, page through the photo galleries on pages 59 through 90 and 187 through 218. You can also look at other garden books and magazines for ideas. You'll find pictures of everything from cottage gardens and old-fashioned Victorian-style gardens to wildflower gardens and modern-looking perennial plantings with ornamental grasses and prairie plants.

WHAT STYLE IS YOUR HOUSE?

Let the style of your house help you pick the style of your garden. Do

Flowers and vines can add appeal to a shed or garage that you don't like the looks of. See how this ordinary-looking shed is dressed up by a trellis covered with clematis and a bed of flowers along its foundation.

you live in a country cottage, an 1790s saltbox colonial, a log cabin, a suburban split level, a contemporary steel-and-glass home? Is your home made of brick or covered with clapboard or another form of siding?

Your home's architectural style doesn't have to dictate the style of garden you plant, but your garden and your home should look appealing together. For example, if you have a contemporary home, a modern-looking garden with bold shapes and colors would be one option. Your

home would probably look equally appealing with an informal woodland garden or surrounded by free-form beds of sun-loving perennials. On the other hand, a stylized Victorian planting scheme would probably look out of place.

If you're not sure what styles look good together, try looking at houses with similar architecture and the gardens that surround them. Make some notes about which features you like and which ones you don't. You also may find pictures of a style you like in books or magazines.

HOW MUCH TIME CAN YOU DEVOTE TO YOUR GARDEN?

There's nothing more frustrating than putting in a big garden and watching it languish because you simply don't have enough time to care for it. Before you set your sights on planting a giant flower garden all along the side and back fences of your yard, ask yourself how much time you have to work in the garden. Is it one or two hours a week? Can you spend several hours every day? If you're like most people, you'll probably have one or two hours a week to work in a flower garden.

Fortunately, one of the beauties of a flower garden is that caring for it really doesn't take a lot of time. Once you have the garden planted and mulched, you'll find that a little bit of puttering is all it takes to keep it looking its best. And puttering— propping up a wayward stem here and there, cutting off spent blooms, picking flowers to bring indoors, or pulling up a weed or two—is a relaxing way to spend an afternoon or evening. Once you get the gardens that I have designed planted, you will only need to spend an hour or two a week to keep them looking their best.

WHERE CAN YOU GET INSPIRATION?

BOOKS and magazines are wonderful ways to get a good idea of what you want to plant in your flower garden. But there's no substitute for visiting a real flower garden when you want to get really inspired.

Public gardens are one of the best places to see a wide variety of flowers you may not have known about before. The Missouri Botanical Garden and the New York Botanical Garden are just two of the dozens of botanical gardens in the United States. Many public gardens have facilities especially designed for helping home gardeners. They may have displays of

plants particularly suited to your region, gardeners' information services that can answer your questions, guided tours that let you ask experts about all the plants you see, and much more.

There are also many historic homes that have flower gardens planted around them and are open to the public. To find out about the location of a public garden near you or near where you are traveling this summer, look in the telephone book or ask your librarian for assistance. There are a variety of guides that list public gardens. (See "Recommended Reading" on page 277 for a listing of some.) Most general travel guides, such as the ones distributed by the American Automobile Association (AAA), also list public gardens.

Garden tours are another good way to learn about flowers. There seems to be a new garden tour springing up every day somewhere in the country. These tours are often put together by a not-for-profit group with the proceeds going to a charity. Typically, people open their private homes and gardens to their neighbors and you get to stroll around the gardens, talk with the owners, and learn what plants grow really well in your area. Don't forget that you can also take your own garden "tour." You'd be surprised what a stroll through the neighborhood can turn up!

Plant sales are another great way to learn about flowers. Put on by local garden clubs, schools, and garden societies, plant sales are full of perennial plants that people have dug up from their own gardens and donated to the sale. Again, you can talk to the sellers to learn where to plant and how to take care of the plants they're offering. You'll also be able to collect lots of information about other plants that grow well in your area.

GROW ALONG WITH YOUR GARDEN

AS YOU PLAN and plant your first garden, always remember that there is no such thing as failure in gardening. Every gardener has lost a tree or perennial they planted. If you try something out and it doesn't work, you can always change it. The most important thing is to relax and have fun. Gardening is good exercise. It's a fun family activity, and you can meet a lot of really wonderful people by visiting with them and asking for their advice. So dig in and have a great time!

CHAPTER THREE

Tooling Up

Tools for a Beautiful Easy Garden

THERE'S NOTHING WORSE than getting yourself all psyched up to work in the garden and then have your trowel bend and break the first time you push it into the soil. After all, gardening should be fun, not frustrating. With a few carefully chosen tools, it can be easy, too. Catalogs and garden centers are filled with all kinds of tools. Some are invaluable in the garden; others just get in the way.

Believe me, I've used the wrong tool lots of times, which caused me to do more work than I wanted to do and to put up with untold hours of aggravation. After years of experimenting, I've settled on a few carefully selected tools that I think will help you grow the best flower garden you've ever had.

The tools in this chapter are divided into three groups: earth movers, including shovels and rakes; small hand tools, including trowels and pruners; and watering tools, including soaker hoses. I'll also tell you how to select and buy a good tool and how to take care of your tools once you have them.

But first I want to let you in on a couple of trade secrets. These two simple tips will make your gardening easier. First, buy the best tool you can afford. And second, use it to do the job it was made for.

How to Choose a Good Tool

POOR-QUALITY tools make gardening harder, not easier, so do yourself a favor and just say "no" to cheap tools. The bottom line is that you want tools that are strong and durable, not flimsy and cheap. Price, size, weight, and construction are the most important factors to consider when buying tools. Before you buy any tool, always look for and demand a full-replacement, multiyear guarantee.

Price: You Get What You Pay For

With tools, you get what you pay for. In most cases, higher-priced tools are better than cheaper ones. I'm not saying you should spend hundreds of dollars on a gold-plated shovel, but better tools are made from better-quality parts, better steel, and better wood. And they're better assembled, too. These factors all cost money, so be prepared to spend a little more to get the very best.

If you have a limited budget for tools, don't despair. You can garden successfully with many fewer tools than the ones I list here. If I had to name just three tools you really need, I would recommend that you buy a long-handled garden spade, a trowel, and a watering can. Those three tools are enough to plant and care for any of the gardens in this book.

One way to beat the high cost of good-quality tools is to shop for them at yard sales. You can often pick up saws, pruning shears, shovels, and other garden tools at a fraction of the cost you'd have to pay for the same tools new. Just make sure you check the quality as well as the price.

Sizing Up Your Tools

Basically, you want to buy tools that have heft. But there is no sense getting a tool that isn't the right size for you. Most tools come in varying weights and sizes, and you can find one that's right for you, whatever your size. Shovels, for example, are made with handles in a variety of lengths. They're also constructed of a variety of materials, which affect the overall weight. If you can, try to buy your tools in person—especially if you're buying a tool with a long handle. That way you can get the feel of it before you buy and see if it is comfortable for you. Go to the store and pretend to use it by going through the motions you'll use in the garden. Does it feel too heavy or too big and awkward? Does it fit comfortably in your hands?

If you prefer to shop by mail, ask the salesperson on the phone about different handle lengths. Make sure you can return a tool you buy through the mail if the size isn't just right.

BUYING WELL-BUILT TOOLS

Look for tools that are made out of forged or tempered high-carbon steel. Stainless steel tools are also available, and they have the advantage of not rusting. But stainless steel tools cost much more than their carbon steel counterparts and don't hold a sharp edge as well. With a minimal amount of annual maintenance, carbon steel tools will give you good value for your money. Tools made from aluminum are generally not a good idea, unless they're made from an exceptionally strong alloy. They just can't take the workout you are bound to give them.

Most good-quality tools have handles made of straight-grained ash. Ash is the same wood used to make major league baseball bats. It's light, strong, and resilient. Hickory, which is stronger and heavier but less flexible, is used for short-handled tools and some spades and forks. Several tool-makers are now coming out with handles made of fiberglass that are lighter weight and just as strong. Beware of tools with wooden handles that have been painted. That paint can hide a multitude of sins, including knotholes and grain that runs from side to side rather than lengthwise—both invitations to splitting.

A wheelbarrow makes it easy to cart everything you need out to the garden in one trip.

EARTH MOVERS

EARTH MOVERS are the tools that let you really get down in the dirt. My selection includes a trusty wheelbarrow, long-handled garden spade, spading fork, and soil rake. In addition, I find a short-handled spade, mattock, and lawn rake are useful in special situations. Let's review each type of tool and how to use it.

WHEELBARROWS SAVE TIME — AND TRIPS

Over the years, I've struggled with enough buckets and bushel baskets to recommend that you absolutely need a wheelbarrow. There simply isn't an easier way to carry dirt, mulch, and other organic matter to a garden. Wheelbarrows are also handy for removing debris and leaves from the garden, as well as for transporting plants and tools. I have a lightweight steel 4-cubic-foot wheelbarrow with wooden handles and a rubber tire. I find that it is very maneuverable, and I can use it to carry all the weight I want to haul at one time. I've found that a construction-grade wheelbarrow, which is larger and heavier than mine, is too much tool for the jobs I need to do in my garden.

MY MOST USEFUL TOOL — A LONG-HANDLED SPADE

My long-handled garden spade is the most useful tool I have — it's the first one I grab when I head for the garden. A good garden spade has a carbon steel blade that's rectangular and fairly flat with a squared-off point. It's perfect for a whole host of gardening chores: digging holes to plant shrubs or bulbs, scraping sod off a new planting area, transplanting and dividing perennials, and turning

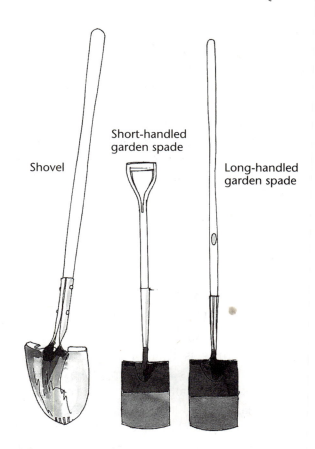

Shovel

Short-handled garden spade

Long-handled garden spade

Whether you like the long- or short-handled model, a garden spade is handy for a variety of chores, including digging and dividing perennials and turning over new soil. A spade is better for gardening than a shovel because it has a sharp, flat blade that is good for cutting through roots. A shovel has a curved blade that comes to a slight point at the tip.

over new soil and breaking it up. You can also use it to scoop compost out of your pile or bin into a wheelbarrow and then scatter it over the soil.

THE SHORT-HANDLED GARDEN SPADE

This tool is just like its longer-handled cousin except that it has a shorter handle with a D-shaped grip. I use a short-handled spade when I have to dig in tight areas, such as up close to the house or a tree. Although I use my long-handled spade for most gardening chores, for those of you who prefer shorter handles, this tool can do all the work a long-handled spade can do.

A SPADING FORK FOR TURNING COMPOST OR SOIL

This tool, which has four broad, flat tines, is ideal for digging up garden beds and turning over new soil. It actually cuts into the soil more easily than a tool with a solid blade like a shovel or spade. I also use it as my primary compost-turning tool. Its biggest drawback is that it is not very efficient at digging up perennials or bulbs for transplanting.

SOIL AND LAWN RAKES

You'll need a steel-toothed garden rake for smoothing out garden beds after you have prepared the soil. This soil rake features short steel tines and is ideal for breaking up clumps and smoothing out the soil in a garden after it has been tilled. Two types are

A spading fork, also called a garden fork, cuts into the soil more easily than a solid-bladed tool like a shovel or spade.

available: The bow-head garden rake has a head attached to the handle with two steel bows that provide a spring action. The other type is a square-back or level-head rake, which, not surprisingly, has a flat back like a comb. It generally has a narrower head, shorter teeth, and a shorter handle than a bow-head rake. Select the type that you find most comfortable to use. If you have rocky soil, you'll find that one with wider teeth is easier to use. Be sure to check that the head is made of solid steel and firmly attached to the handle.

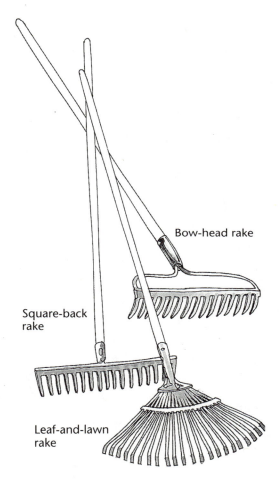

Bow-head rake

Square-back rake

Leaf-and-lawn rake

A steel-toothed garden rake is handy for putting the finishing touches on garden beds. You can choose either a bow-head or square-back garden rake. Use a leaf-and-lawn rake for removing leaves and other debris from your garden beds.

You'll also need a leaf-and-lawn rake from time to time. The only time you really need one is to rake leaves and other debris out of your beds in late fall or early spring. I prefer the

lawn rakes with teeth made out of bamboo, although steel teeth do an equally good job. Make sure your plants are dormant before you rake!

THE MATTOCK—A TOUGH TOOL FOR DIGGING JOBS

This is a tool you don't absolutely have to have, but I finally bought my own because I found myself borrowing one to use several times each year. A mattock is a heavy-duty digging tool with a head that has a pick on one end and a blade on the other. I've used my mattock a lot to dig out old bushes, break up stony ground, and clear tree and shrub roots to make room for a trellis or plant I want to put in the ground. A variety of sizes and weights are available. Shop around until you find a store that offers several sizes. Then try them out and decide which size and weight is most comfortable for you.

Using a mattock takes a bit of practice, but if you have a tough digging challenge ahead of you, it's worth the effort to learn. To use one, hold it as you would an axe, with one hand near the bottom of the handle and the other hand higher up to steady it. Then raise it over your head and swing it down into the ground. Try to let gravity do most of the work and just guide the mattock into the

A mattock is useful for heavy-duty digging chores. When you use one, bend at the knees, with one foot in front of the other, and keep your lower back straight. Don't force the blade into the ground by putting pressure on your back and spine. Instead, let gravity add strength to your swing, and you can concentrate on simply controlling the tool as it falls.

ground; don't force it into the ground with your back and arms. By the way, a mattock is one of the more dangerous tools in the gardener's arsenal. Don't use one when you're tired or for such a long digging session that you become careless. It's too easy to make a mistake and hurt yourself.

SMALL HAND TOOLS

YOU'LL never use any garden tool more often than your trowel. In fact, a trowel is so indispensable in the flower garden that you may find you need more than one type. I like another hand tool, too—the hand fork. It's great for breaking up soil in a bed. Read on for more about these gardening mainstays.

TROWELS — THE INDISPENSABLE TOOLS

The important thing to remember about a trowel is that if you buy a poorly made one, it is going to bend when you use it. And it will keep on bending until it breaks. Instead of settling on a tool that's going to be nearly useless and annoying to use, look for a heavy-duty trowel with a steel blade and shank forged in one piece. Forged steel trowels should have hardwood handles. There are also sturdy trowels cast in one piece from aluminum alloy with cushioned grip handles.

Trowels come in two sizes, and I use them both. I use a trowel with a wider blade for digging holes and transplanting larger plants. One with a slightly narrower blade is better for transplanting smaller, more delicate plants in tight places such as a rock garden.

Hand fork

Wide-bladed
trowel

Narrow-
bladed trowel

A hand fork is useful for breaking up soil in a small area. A wide-bladed trowel is great for most flower-planting chores, while a narrow-bladed trowel is handy for working in tight spaces, such as between stones in a rock garden .

A HAND FORK— HANDY FOR PLANTING

Sometimes when I am working in a fairly new bed where the soil is not fully broken up, I find myself reaching for my three-pronged hand fork to get the job done. This tool looks something like a miniature spading fork but is used more like a trowel. Use it to loosen the soil and break up small clods when you are planting. Be sure you get a hand fork; a hand cultivator has curved tines and will not help you dig up soil.

PRUNING TOOLS

As YOU might guess, pruning isn't a major focus when you're making a flower garden. But a good pair of pruning shears can come in handy if you grow perennials and roses. And you never know when you might have to limb up a tree, thin out a shrub, or cut down a badly placed woody plant to make room for your garden. Luckily, with the right tools, pruning isn't hard. Here's a look at the three essential pruning tools— pruning shears, loppers, and a folding saw.

PRUNING SHEARS FOR EVERY PLANT

If you grow flowering shrubs, perennials, or roses, you will need a pair of pruning shears. Look for forged steel cutting blades that bypass each other like scissors when they cut. This gives a smoother, cleaner cut than anvil types, which crush stems against a flat blade when cutting. Both you and your plants will appreciate the difference. Try to find pruning shears that have replaceable blades. There's nothing more wasteful than having to replace an entire pair of pruning shears because the blades are no longer sharp. Felco and Sandvik are two brands with replaceable parts.

Bypass loppers

Bypass pruning shears

Folding pruning saw

You don't need anything fancy to prune effectively. You will be able to tackle any pruning chore with these three tools—bypass loppers, bypass pruning shears, and a folding pruning saw.

Pruning shears come in a variety of sizes and are available for both right- and left-handed gardeners. Look for a pair that is comfortable in your hand. If you have small hands, buy smaller pruners so you can open and close them comfortably.

LOPPERS TAKE A BITE OUT OF BIG SHRUBS

Loppers or lopping shears are handy if you have mature shrubs in or near your flower garden that might shade your flowers or if you have to clear mature shrubs to make a garden. Look for steel bypass blades and strong wooden or aluminum handles. You don't need the ratchet-type loppers, which are more expensive than the standard type, because you won't be cutting anything so large that you will need the extra force.

A FOLDING PRUNING SAW FOR THE BIG JOBS

Once again, you won't need this tool often, but when you do, it's handy to have on hand. Use a pruning saw to remove tree and shrub branches that are too large for your loppers. This type of saw has a 6- or 7-inch saw-toothed blade that folds into a wooden or plastic handle. The blade is then screwed into place so you can't accidentally cut your hand on the blade when you're reaching for it or another tool. If you're not sure whether to use a pruning saw or loppers for a particular task, it's generally best to use a pruning saw. That's because you can damage a shrub or tree if you start to remove a branch with loppers, only to find that the branch is simply too large. It's much better to saw the limb off cleanly in the first place.

WATERING TOOLS

A WATERING CAN is one of my three indispensable tools. But if you have more than a small bed to water, you'll find that hoses save a lot of running around. A soaker hose is the ultimate easy tool, since you just put it in place, then turn it on as needed. But sometimes, nothing beats an old-fashioned garden hose for getting the job done—and cooling off afterward! But you can find out more about watering the right way—how, when, and with what—in Chapter 5.

YOUR BASIC WATERING CAN

I think a 3- to 5-gallon galvanized steel watering can is one of the best tools to use to water newly planted seedbeds or new transplants. For one thing, it allows you to control the direction and flow of the water more accurately than you can with a hose. It is also good for watering potted plants on terraces, patios, or other places you don't want to drag a hose.

A soaker hose delivers water directly to plant roots. It is much more efficient and effective than a conventional overhead sprinkler. The easiest way to use it is to snake it through the garden at the beginning of the season and cover it with mulch. Leave the connecting end of the soaker hose handy so you can attach a conventional garden hose to it when you need to water.

SOAKER HOSE—THE BEST WAY TO WATER

Once your garden is growing, the best way to water it is with a soaker hose. It is made out of porous rubber that "weeps" water out over its entire length. (Soaker hoses are often made of recycled rubber tires.) A soaker hose is very effective at conserving water because it delivers water directly to the soil and to the roots of your plants instead of watering the leaves and the area around them.

A soaker hose is easy to use, too. Just snake it through your flower garden at planting time by placing it next to each plant you'd like to water. Cover it with mulch, and leave it in place throughout the season. When you need to water, all you do is attach a conventional hose to one end, turn the water on to very low pressure, and let it seep slowly into the soil.

A HOST OF USES FOR THE GARDEN HOSE

You will need a heavy-duty conventional hose to run water from the spigot to the soaker hose, which remains in place in the garden during the growing season. (You can't connect a soaker hose directly to the spigot because it drips all along its length.) A conventional hose is also valuable for direct spot soaking of large perennials and shrubs when they are newly planted or just in need of heavy watering.

Don't waste your time with a cheap plastic hose that kinks and tangles at the drop of a hat. Either buy a rubber hose or one of the new, no-kink hoses that are made of nylon-reinforced rubber and vinyl.

HOW TO "HARVEST" FREE WATER

ALL YOU NEED to harvest hundreds of gallons of free water each year is a rain barrel attached to a downspout of your gutter system. I use a hard plastic recycled pickle barrel with a porous removable top, but any wooden barrel or metal washtub will work. You need to have a lid on it so that mosquitoes don't move in during the summer.

If you like, you can buy rain barrels that have spigots attached, which you can either use to fill a watering can or attach directly to a hose. (If you are going to use the hose option, your garden will need to be downhill from your barrel.)

HOW TO TAKE CARE OF YOUR TOOLS

THE BEST THING you can do to extend the useful life of your tools is to keep them clean. Your goal is to prevent rust buildup on the steel blades, prongs, tines, shanks, and handles of your tools. Always knock all the dirt off of your tools and thoroughly wipe the steel blades clean and dry after each use. You should also wipe the blades with a slightly oily rag after each use. Be sure to wipe the handles and remove any dirt or moisture from them, too. Once or twice a year, wipe the wooden handles down with a rag slightly moistened with linseed oil to protect the wood.

Be sure to wipe the blades of your pruning shears, too. Many shrubs and plants contain juices that can gum up your blades. It is a good idea to keep them oiled as well.

Another thing you can do to take care of your tools is to keep them in the right place. I keep all of my hand tools in a small canvas bag, and I have specially marked spots in my garage where I hang all the larger tools on the wall. This way I always know where they are and don't waste time looking all over creation for them.

CHAPTER FOUR

Don't Treat Your Soil like Dirt

A Guide to Caring for Your Soil

THE BIGGEST MISTAKE most beginning gardeners make when they start a new flower garden is to treat their soil like dirt. All too often they scratch up a couple of inches of soil, toss down some kind of chemical fertilizer, put the plants in the ground, and wait for pretty flowers to happen. When the flowers wilt and die in the summer sun or are attacked by bugs, they wonder what went wrong.

The problem is they haven't given the soil the respect it deserves. Think of your soil as a gardening partner. If you care for it properly, it will support and feed your plants for you. In this chapter, I'll tell you how to build and care for soil that will support beautiful flowers with a minimum of effort from you. You will also learn how to dig and prepare a bed for planting.

I can promise you that spending the time and money to prepare your soil right the first time, before you plant anything, will pay dividends for a long time to come. Poor soil is more difficult to improve once you have planted your flower bed, especially if you planted shrubs, perennials, or roses. And well-prepared soil will grow fabulous flowers that are healthy and trouble-free with very little work from you.

Good soil care is based on adding organic matter to your soil. This creates a loose, porous "sponge" that holds water and nutrients for your plants' roots to take up. There are plenty of kinds of organic matter, but compost is my favorite hands down. See page 41 for compost that makes itself.

WHAT IS SOIL?

GOOD garden soil, the kind you want to have, is a fascinating mix of ingredients—it's far more than just dirt. Good soil contains rock particles like sand, silt, and clay, along with organic matter, water, air, and even creatures like earthworms and microorganisms. In an average sampling of soil, about 45 percent is rock particles and about 5 percent is organic matter. The other half of the soil is open spaces, called pore spaces, that are filled with water and air. Microorganisms and other soil life feed on soil organic matter and break it down into nutrients that will feed your plants.

Your first job as a gardener is to make sure that the microorganisms in your soil stay happy and well fed. They in turn will feed your plants for you. Your other major job is to make sure your soil is a good place for roots to grow. To do that effectively, it helps to know a little bit about the rock particles in your soil, the kinds of organic matter, and the pore spaces in soil that provide roots and microorganisms with the air and water they need.

ROCK PARTICLES: THE "DIRT" IN SOIL

There are three kinds of rock particles in soil: sand, silt, and clay. The amount of each type of particle in your soil will affect how plants will grow in it. It also determines some of the problems you may have.

Here's an easy way to find out what kinds of particles are in your soil: Pick up a handful of moistened soil and squeeze it in your hand. Then release it and gently press it with your thumb. If it won't form a ball at all and the sample feels gritty against your palm when you rub it with your thumb, your soil is sandy. If the sample crumbles when you gently press it, you have a good mix of particles in your soil. If the sample holds its ball shape under gentle pressure, your soil has quite a bit of clay in it. If you can roll it into a sausage shape, it has even more clay.

If you have a good mix of particles, relax. You are the envy of all those gardeners out there who are coping with sandy or clay soil. All you need to do to keep your garden thriving is add organic matter to your soil and keep it mulched.

If you're a gardener with soil that is high in sand or clay, you'll also want to add organic matter—lots of it. That's because organic matter will help a sandy soil hold water better and make a clay soil easier to dig. See "Soil Type Tips" on page 40 for more on managing these two types of soil.

SOIL TYPE TIPS

USE THESE SUGGESTIONS to manage your soil more effectively.

Sandy Soil

Soil that has lots of sand drains very quickly and can't hold much moisture for plant roots. Adding organic matter will fix both these problems, but you need to add lots of it every year. Microorganisms in sandy soil eat up organic matter much faster than they do in clay soil. If you have very sandy soil, when you plant the gardens in Part 2, add twice as much organic matter as I recommend. In addition, if you can avoid it, don't redig your gardens each year because that only uses up organic matter faster. Instead, spread organic matter and mulch on the top of the soil each year and plant into that. Earthworms and other soil animals will move the new organic matter down into the soil for you.

Clay Soil

Sticky, slippery, hard-to-dig clay is a gardener's nightmare, but clay soils do have their good side. They are very rich in nutrients, and if you add enough organic matter, they are perfect for growing flowers. Clay soils tend to stay wet and cold in spring, and if you work them when they are too wet, they will form rock-hard clumps. Before you dig in a clay soil—or any soil for that matter—always test to see if it is too wet. If a handful of soil forms a sticky, muddy clump, wait a few days and test it again. Even if you live in a subdivision where all the topsoil was removed when the houses were built, you can still have a beautiful easy garden. The best way is to build raised beds. You can use timber framing to make sides for your bed. Then fill it with a mixture of good topsoil and organic matter like compost or shredded leaves.

ORGANIC MATTER— A GARDENER'S BEST FRIEND

Organic matter holds moisture in the soil and feeds the microorganisms that feed your plants. Making and using compost is one of the best ways to add soil organic matter. See the illustration on the opposite page for a no-nonsense way to make compost for your garden. If you don't have time or room to make your own compost, compost and composted manure are both available at your local garden center and are good sources of organic matter. If you are preparing a garden bed in the fall for planting the following spring, you can also add chopped leaves, grass clippings, and even kitchen scraps directly to the soil and dig them in. In spring when you are ready to plant, they will have decomposed. Organic mulches like shredded bark also add organic matter to the soil as they break down.

PORE SPACE— ROOM FOR AIR AND WATER

Most people are astonished to find that half of healthy soil is actually pore space. Ideally, half of the pores in soil are large spaces filled with air, and half are small spaces that hold water. When it rains, all the spaces are filled with water for a time. Ideally, the large spaces drain fairly quickly, reestablishing a balance between air and water. Clay soils have too many small pore spaces and don't drain well; sandy soils have too many large ones, and the water seems to run right through them.

Soil pores are formed as the soil freezes and thaws, roots grow and die, and earthworms tunnel. Ideally, all these forces cause rock particles and soil organic matter to clump together to make plenty of space for air between them. When you add organic matter to your garden, you are helping this process and making your soil a better place for plant roots and earthworms to live.

To protect the pore spaces in your soil, try to avoid walking on prepared garden beds. Why? Every time you do, you compress the large pores that

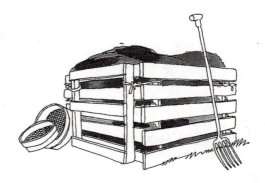

Making compost doesn't have to be complicated. Add materials until your pile is 3 feet tall, then start a new pile. You can leave a finished pile alone, wait about a year, and it will turn into compost without any help from you. To speed things up, keep the pile moist (*not* soggy) and turn it every two to four weeks with a garden fork. Turning adds air to the pile and keeps microorganisms actively decomposing its ingredients.

let air in. Try to tend your flowers from the sides of the beds rather than walking directly in the beds, or add stepping stones or paths to make maintenance easier. Tilling your soil repeatedly—especially when it is dry—also destroys pore space by pulverizing the soil clumps.

FEED THE SOIL, NOT THE PLANTS

As LONG as you keep adding organic matter to your soil, you won't have to pour on tons of fertilizer to keep your plants healthy. Adding organic matter in the form of compost or composted

COMPOST DOS AND DON'TS

ALL YOU NEED to do to make compost the easy way is to add a variety of the ingredients listed here to your bin or pile.

DO ADD:

Kitchen scraps, including eggshells, fruit and vegetable peelings, coffee grounds, and tea leaves

Grass clippings

Garden trimmings, including dead leaves, flowers, and flowerstalks

Chopped leaves, weed-free straw, sawdust, and shredded newspaper

Weeds, but not ones that have set seed

DON'T ADD:

Dog and cat droppings

Meat scraps, bones, or grease

Diseased plant parts

Weed seeds

When you buy, read the package and look for words like "certified organic" or "natural organic." The three-number ratio on the label, which tells you the amounts of nitrogen, phosphorus, and potassium in the package, should be 5-5-5 or thereabouts.

Don't buy chemical fertilizers for your garden. The salts in them drive away earthworms and decrease all the microorganism activity you've worked so hard to encourage. Chemical fertilizers also leach out of the soil and into our waterways, creating major pollution problems.

GETTING YOUR GARDEN READY TO PLANT

NOW THAT you know the basics of how your soil works, you are ready to prepare your garden bed. You can prepare garden beds in the spring or fall. If you do it in the spring, try to get the soil ready a few weeks before you are ready to plant. Or do your digging in the fall, mulch the bed over winter, and you'll be ready to plant in the spring.

Start by marking off your site with stakes and string or sprinkling the edges with flour. Then use a garden spade to skim off any grass on the site, as shown on page 44. You can

manure regularly will feed the microorganisms in your soil. In turn, they will keep your flowers fed.

This doesn't mean you should shun all fertilizers, though. I recommend giving your garden an annual feeding to give it a boost. You can buy a general-purpose, balanced organic fertilizer for this and apply it according to the package directions.

use the grass you've skimmed off to repair patchy parts of your lawn. Otherwise, turn it upside down on your compost pile or somewhere else that's out of the way where it can break down.

If there are lots of weeds on your site, it's a good idea to take the time to dig them out. A mattock is a handy tool for digging up roots of woody plants; try a garden fork to loosen the soil around dandelions or weedy grasses so you can pull them up roots and all. (See Chapter 3 for more on these and other garden tools.) That way, you don't have to worry about them coming back and competing with your flowers. Don't worry too much about small weeds—a thick layer of mulch will take care of them. Just concentrate on removing large, vigorous weeds.

TEST THE SOIL

Chances are, if plants are growing well in your yard already, your soil will be fine for growing flowers. If you aren't sure what condition your soil is in or if you would like to know more about your soil, it's a good idea to have a soil test done. Your local Cooperative Extension Service office offers this service for a small fee. (Look for their listing under city or county governments in your tele-phone book.) They will have a kit available that includes all the instructions you need to collect a soil sample and have the test done. (In some areas, you can pick up a kit at your local library.) Follow their directions to collect a sample from the area you would like to plant. Indicate what you would like to grow, and be sure to ask for organic recommendations.

Your soil test will recommend fertilizer applications and tell you the pH of your soil. Soil pH is a measure of how acid or alkaline your soil is. It's measured on a scale of 1.0 to

---

DON'T SKIP THIS TEST!

NO MATTER HOW anxious you are to get your garden planted, always take a minute to see if your soil is ready to work. Pick up a handful of soil. If it's ready, it should crumble easily in your hand. If it's sticky or wet enough to make a ball, wait a few days and try again. If it is so dry that it turns to dust in your hand, water the site thoroughly and wait a day or so before you dig. Digging your soil when it's too wet or too dry will de-stroy all the soil pores that plant roots and microorganisms need to breathe.

To remove lawn grass from a site, cut around the edges of a long narrow strip. Then skim the grass and roots off with a sharp spade, roll up the strip, and use the sod for patching bare spots in the lawn.

Annual applications of organic matter actually tend to bring your soil into the ideal 6.0 to 7.0 range. In fact, if your soil tests anywhere between 5.5 and 7.8, you probably don't need to do anything more to adjust pH than add organic matter. If your soil is either more acid or more alkaline than this, follow your soil test recommendations for adjusting pH. Use ground dolomitic limestone to raise pH; add sulfur to lower it. It's best to adjust pH gradually over several years.

ADD THE AMENDMENTS

Once you have removed the grass and weeds on your site, spread on compost and any other organic matter that you are going to add to the soil. For the gardens in this book, you will need about four wheelbarrows full of compost. When spread out over the whole garden, that's about a 1-inch-thick layer. (You can't really add too much compost, so if you have more available, by all means add it. It's a good idea to add extra compost if you have very sandy or very clayey soil.) If you don't have that much homemade compost, buy bags of prepared compost, composted manure, or dehydrated manure. You can also add shredded leaves or strawy manure if you are preparing your bed in the fall. Don't use fresh manure if you are

14.0, with 7.0 being neutral, 1.0 being extremely acid, and 14.0 being extremely alkaline. Most flowers grow best with a pH of 6.0 to 7.0, which is slightly acid to neutral. They'll grow in a wider range than that, but that is the ideal range where most plants thrive.

going to plant right away because it can burn young plants.

Then spread any soil amendments to adjust pH, as recommended by your soil test. I also recommend spreading a balanced organic fertilizer—a 5-pound bag is all you need for any of the gardens in this book.

JUST DIG IN

Once you've spread the organic matter, amendments, and fertilizer, you need to dig the soil to at least 6 inches to work all these goodies into the soil. Digging also helps loosen the soil and create air space for roots and soil microorganisms. If you really want to accomplish this task the easy way, hire a person with a rotary tiller to come over to your house and till your site. It will take about 30 minutes to an hour and cost less than $50. You can also borrow a rotary tiller from a friend or neighbor, or rent one for a day and split the cost with other gardening friends who need their beds tilled also.

Digging by hand is a lot of hard work, especially the first year. But it's good exercise, and many gardeners enjoy hand-digging garden beds.

After you have tilled or hand-dug your flower bed, grab your steel-toothed garden rake and smooth out the surface of your bed. Rake out any

stones or large debris that might have been turned up. If you dug by hand, use the rake to break up any clumps and leave your bed with a smooth, crumbly, and level planting surface. That's all there is to it—now you are ready to plant.

If you use a rotary tiller to prepare your site, make several passes. Set the tiller at the most shallow depth setting to start, then increase the depth with each pass until you have worked the soil at least 8 inches deep.

Plant Care Made Easy

Simple Techniques
for Keeping Your Garden Beautiful

CARING FOR YOUR GARDEN doesn't have to mean an endless parade of chores. Obviously, you do need to care for your flowers—watering when rain doesn't fall regularly, mulching to prevent weeds, and taking steps to keep pests and diseases at bay. But with the simple low-maintenance plan of action outlined in this chapter, you will be spending more time enjoying your beautiful easy flowers than struggling with chores.

That's because when you make a beautiful easy garden, you design a garden that takes care of itself. First, you choose plants that will grow well where you want to put them. (This part is *easy*—the 11 gardens in Part 2 are geared toward particular sites in your yard, like a sunny bed or a fence or wall.) Then you lay down a soaker hose in the bed, so watering is as easy as turning on the tap. Next, you put down a thick layer of organic mulch to cut down on weeding and watering. And finally, you encourage birds, toads, and beneficial insects to visit your garden and take care of pest problems. (Didn't I say this was easy?) Read on to find out how to make your garden work for you instead of vice-versa.

WATERING YOUR GARDEN

OF COURSE, your flowers need water to grow vigorously and look their best. But they aren't the only things in your garden that need water. Earthworms and soil microorganisms need it, too. (Earthworms tunnel through the soil and improve soil conditions for plant roots, and microorganisms break down organic matter to feed your plants, remember?)

You may not have realized it at the time, but when you prepared your garden site, you weren't just getting ready to plant your garden. You were also helping to create soil that holds lots of water and stays moist longer than ordinary garden soil. Soil that has lots of organic matter in it, like the soil in your garden after you've prepared it, acts like a sponge and holds water ready for plants to use. (For more on how organic matter functions, read "What Is Soil?" on page 39.)

Plants growing in soil that is rich in organic matter generally won't need watering as often as plants growing in unimproved soil. But you'll still need to water your garden when rainfall is scanty.

SOAKER HOSES— EASY AND EFFICIENT

I recommend using soaker hoses in beautiful easy flower gardens be-

When you install a soaker hose, be careful not to accidentally damage new plants. Warming the hose in the sun before you put it down makes it easier to handle. Hold it in place with rocks or plant stakes as you position it so it doesn't get dragged over plants by mistake. Be sure to position the connecting end on the side of your garden nearest the spigot.

Since a soaker hose will drench the ground 12 to 18 inches on either side of the hose, it's not necessary to place it right next to each and every plant.

cause they are practical and efficient—both in terms of your time and of the water you put on your garden. A soaker hose drips water all along its length, letting it ooze down to plant roots. Since you can spread it anywhere you like, you can position a soaker hose right next to your plants. That means no water is wasted on weeds or paths. Unlike overhead sprinklers, soaker hoses don't waste lots of water because of evaporation either. (On a hot summer day, a lot of the water that overhead sprinklers deliver evaporates before it hits the ground.) The easiest way to use soaker hoses is to spread them through your gardens and leave them

in place all season. You can buy soaker hoses at your local garden center or through mail-order catalogs.

To install a soaker hose, simply snake it through the flower garden in an extended S-pattern, so that the moisture will soak out to reach most of the plants. Running a hose between rows of plants or down the center of a free-form grouping is a good option. During the growing season, adjust the placement if you notice an area that doesn't seem to be getting enough water.

If you planted your garden with container-grown perennials, bareroot roses, and/or annuals in 2½- or 3-inch pots, you can either water by hand for the first few weeks or spread a soaker hose through the garden as soon as you have finished planting. (You need to water each and every plant when you plant it, but you can use a soaker hose thereafter, if you like.)

When you are growing plants from seed, wait until the seedlings are 3 to 5 inches tall and you have thinned them to their final spacing before laying down a soaker hose.

DECIDING WHEN TO WATER

A new garden needs to be watered frequently, whether you have sown seeds or planted container-grown or bareroot plants. See "Watering

Seedlings" on this page for my recommendation for getting seeds off to a good start. If you've planted bareroot or container-grown plants, water every other day or every third day for best results. New annuals, perennials, roses, shrubs, and vines need water to become established and begin to grow. After all, transplanting is stressful business! Soil that is too dry can damage roots and slow plant growth.

Wilting is a signal that plants need water *now*. Once you see signs that the plants are growing, reduce your watering schedule slightly. Check the soil every other day and water every third or fourth day—whenever the top ½ inch or so of soil becomes dried out. (Check the soil with your finger to see how moist it is before you water. If it has rained, you may not need to water at all.) Continue to reduce the number of times you water and increase the length of each watering session until you are watering weekly.

WATERING SEEDLINGS

FRESHLY PLANTED SEEDS need to be kept constantly moist until they germinate and are growing strongly. I suggest you use an ordinary watering can for this task. (With a garden hose, it is far too easy to blast the seeds out of the soil.) Lightly water your seedbeds every day until seedlings emerge. You only need to drizzle on enough water to moisten the bed to a depth of ½ to 1 inch. Just a little!

Once the seedlings are up and growing and are about 1 to 2 inches tall, cut back on the watering to once or twice a week, assuming there is no unusual drought and the seedlings look healthy. You can water young annual or perennial transplants the same way if

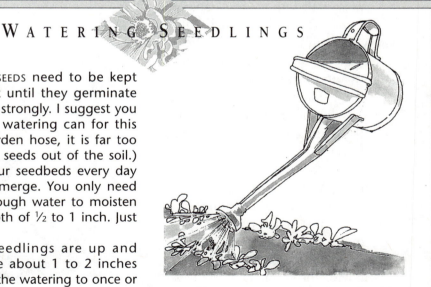

you like—once or twice a week with a watering can—until they are growing strongly. After that, install a soaker hose to make watering easy.

Once the plants are established and growing strongly, you can relax a bit. If your garden has received ½ to 1 inch or more of rain during the week, don't water at all. If it has been a dry week, hook your conventional garden hose to the soaker hose that runs through your garden. Then turn on the spigot—a quarter or half turn of the spigot will deliver all the water a soaker hose needs to work effectively. The water needs to seep out—not shoot out!

Let the hose run for two hours. This weekly, two-hour soaking should moisten the ground to a depth of about 4 to 6 inches, which is just what you want. Don't run the soaker hose again for at least another seven days. It's important for the soil to dry out a little before you water again. This encourages plant roots to dig deep into the soil in search of water. Strong, deep roots make for healthier plants.

That's really all there is to watering. You leave the soaker hose in the garden, under the mulch, all summer. Run it once a week, maximum, and forget about it. No deciding which sprinkler to buy. No moving the sprinkler around every few minutes and getting soaked when you do. No water running down the driveway. Easy, huh?

MAGICAL, WORK-SAVING MULCH

DON'T THINK of mulching your garden as a chore you have to do. Instead, think of it as an easy, one-step way to save yourself lots of other garden chores. Organic mulch—compost, chopped leaves, pine bark, cocoa hulls, buckwheat hulls, whatever you have available—is very beneficial for your garden. A layer of mulch will almost completely stifle weeds. It also acts as a blanket to keep moisture in the soil and keep it

Spread mulch up to, but not touching, plant stems. Mulch piled against plant stems can cause stem and crown rot.

cool, which makes your plants happy. Mulch also protects your soil from wind and rain erosion, keeps soil from splashing up onto your flowers, and actually helps prevent soilborne diseases from infecting your plants. Finally, organic mulch decomposes over the course of a growing season and adds organic matter to the soil, improving it in the process. That's a lot to accomplish by mulching the garden once a year, isn't it?

Notice I don't recommend black plastic or landscape fabric. Neither improves the soil, although each will keep weeds down. My personal mulch favorite is a combination of compost, composted horse manure mixed with bedding, and shredded cedar bark. I think it has a nice woodland look, and since I make my own compost and a horse named Flash lives next door, the only material I have to buy is the shredded cedar.

Mulch gardens planted with bareroot or container-grown plants right after you've finished planting and spread your soaker hose. For seed-grown plantings, wait until the plants have several sets of leaves and have been thinned to their final spacing. When you mulch, cover the garden, soaker hose and all. (Be sure to leave the end where you connect it to your conventional garden hose uncovered.) For best results, pull or dig any weeds that have popped up in your new bed, then spread a 4- to 6-inch layer of mulch.

MANAGING PLANT DISEASES

THE EASIEST WAY to deal with plant diseases is to prevent them from ever getting a foothold in your garden.

WIPE OUT WEEDING WORRIES

MULCH AND PROPER SOIL PREPARATION will take care of nearly all your weeding worries. Digging out grass and weed roots when you prepare your site eliminates most major weeds. Mulch will prevent weed seeds in the soil from germinating. Any weeds that do germinate will be more than likely growing with their roots in the mulch, so they'll be easy to pull with a flick of the wrist. Even weeds that have their roots in the soil should be easy to control: They're easily pulled by hand because the soil is so loose and moist. You have no need to own a hoe, much less break your back using one.

That's really not as complicated as it sounds. In fact, you've already done most of the work it takes to keep diseases at bay. For one thing, healthy flowers growing in well-prepared soil are not particularly prone to being attacked by diseases. Soil that drains well and has plenty of pore spaces for air and water discourages rots and wilts. Mulch keeps disease spores that overwinter in the soil from splashing onto your plants and getting a foothold. A fresh layer of mulch helps prevent diseases like powdery and downy mildew.

Another important line of defense is to plant flowers that are naturally resistant or immune to diseases. Whenever possible, the garden designs in Part 2 feature flowers that are naturally disease-resistant. Even if you love roses, I'm sure you don't love blackspot, mildew, and other rose diseases. You'll find plenty of suggestions for great-looking, long-blooming roses that you'll never have to spray in my "Beautiful Easy Roses" design on page 119.

Providing adequate sunlight is another easy way to prevent disease problems. A sun-loving plant growing in a site that is too shady will have more problems with diseases than the same plant growing in

a site that receives six to eight hours of full sun per day. If you have a shady site, fill it with shade lovers that will thrive there rather than flowers that will just survive.

Air circulation also helps prevent plant diseases. Overcrowded, dense plantings can create an invitation for problems with powdery and downy mildew, for example. The spacings I have recommended in the designs in Part 2 ensure that air will circulate around plants, thus discouraging diseases. Another way you can improve

Opening up the center of a plant by removing a few stems at the base increases air circulation and reduces disease problems.

air circulation is to thin out dense clumps of plants by removing a few stems at the base each year. This is a good way to help control powdery mildew on phlox, for example.

WHAT TO DO IF DISEASES STRIKE

There are some simple ways to control diseases that do strike. Oftentimes, the tool to reach for isn't a sprayer, it's your pruning shears. You can keep many diseases from spreading by picking off afflicted leaves and pruning away infected stems. Cut into healthy growth, and dispose of the prunings in your garbage can, not your compost pile.

If you see growth that is de-formed, curled, or mottled with yellow or white, suspect a virus. Unfortunately for us and our plants, there isn't a cure for viral diseases, which are spread by aphids and leafhoppers. Pull up afflicted plants and dispose of them to keep the problem from spreading.

Organic fungicides, like fungicidal soap and sulfur sprays or dusts, can stop the spread of a disease. They won't restore growth that's already damaged by diseases, though. But before you start an all-out spray program, consider whether the plant is really being hurt by the disease. If it's not, why ruin your summer by spending a lot of time spraying? If the plant can live with the disease, you probably can, too.

At the end of the season, there are some easy chores you can do to prevent disease problems next year. If you have any plants that were par-ticularly plagued by diseases, learn a bit more about the plants' habits and preferences. Perhaps you could move the plants to another site in the fall or spring—with better soil drainage or more sun, for example—where they would be happier and have fewer problems.

Also take time to rake up leaves and cut back plant stems once winter really sets in. Add the trimmings to the compost pile if diseases haven't been a particular problem this year. Dispose of trimmings you suspect are disease-infected in the garbage.

MANAGING GARDEN PESTS

SERIOUS pest problems are few and far between in a garden that has healthy, vigorously growing plants. Pest in-sects tend to attack flowers that are weak and struggling. Your flowers, which will thrive in the soil you've prepared for them, will shrug off most pest problems without any trouble. (Did you know you actually were taking the first step in controlling garden pests when you prepared your soil?) Keeping your garden mulched and watered also helps control pests because it prevents plants from becoming stressed, which leads to insect infestations.

A great, easy way to keep pests from becoming problems is to encourage beneficial insects and animals to make your yard their home. See "Welcome Beneficials" on this page for tips on encouraging pest-eating insects and animals to move in and control pests for you.

Of course, you will still run into pests in your garden. But before you panic and spray everything in sight, look closely at the plant that's infested and see if the insects are actually causing long-lasting damage. Don't

WELCOME BENEFICIALS

BIRDS, BENEFICIAL INSECTS, AND TOADS will all help you control pests in your garden. Here are some tips for welcoming these hard-working garden helpers.

• Add birdhouses, along with feeders and a birdbath, to encourage birds to set up housekeeping in your yard.

• Don't use pesticides—either chemical ones or botanical sprays and dusts that are organically acceptable. Sprays kill or damage populations of beneficial insects.

• Plant flowers that attract beneficial insects; many are included in the garden designs in Part 2. Plants that attract beneficial insects include bee balm (*Monarda didyma*), coreopsis (*Coreopsis* spp.), goldenrods (*Solidago* spp.), lavenders (*Lavandula* spp.), marigolds (*Tagetes* spp.), sunflowers (*Helianthus* spp.), thymes (*Thymus* spp.), and yarrows (*Achillea* spp.).

• Provide beneficial insects with a shallow "bug bath" that they can drink from without drowning. Fill a shallow dish with stones and keep it filled with water. Make sure there are plenty of dry stones for insects to land on.

• Toads welcome moist and shady spots. Provide them with an overturned flowerpot with a "door" knocked out of the rim that they can call home.

worry about a few holes chomped out of leaves or petals. It's also a good idea to try to identify the insects you see before you take steps to control them. (A color guide to garden pests would come in handy here; see "Recommended Reading" on page 277 for some suggestions.) Many beginning gardeners (and more advanced ones, too) panic at the sight of *anything* moving on their plants and end up "controlling" beneficial insects that were not doing any damage in the first place.

It is best to avoid using sprays and dusts to control pests. Beneficial insects, birds, and other animals will do lots of the controlling for you if you give them time. A strong spray of water from your hose is an effective, nontoxic control, too. Spraying even organically acceptable insecticides can harm populations of the very beneficials that are trying to help you. If you do decide to use sprays like pyrethrum or neem, always read the manufacturer's directions carefully. Do not leave them around where kids or pets might get in to them. Spray in the very early morning or late evening when bees and butterflies are less likely to be in your garden.

Here's a rundown of the major pests that you may encounter in your garden and the easiest, least-toxic ways to control them.

APHIDS — JUST WASH 'EM OFF

Aphids are tiny (⅕ inch), pale green, beige, reddish, or blue-black insects that cluster at stem tips, on flower buds, and under leaves. They are especially a problem in early spring and love roses and lupines. Fortunately, lady beetles—better known as ladybugs—love aphids, which is one of the reasons lady beetles are so welcome in gardens. The rather alarming-looking larvae of lady

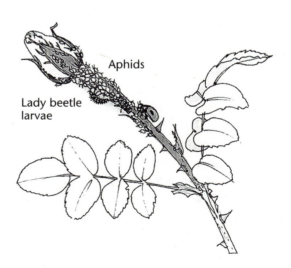

Lady beetle larvae look alarming, but they will eat as many or more aphids than their parents do.

beetles will eat their share of aphids, too. Concentrate your efforts on attracting lady beetles to your garden rather than going out and buying a bag of them. The lady beetles sold in garden centers generally fly away when released. Once aphids are out in spring, the lady beetles are usually not far behind.

A good way to control aphids is to use your hose and simply spray them off the plants with a stiff stream of water. Spray every three or four days until the populations are under control. Use insecticidal soap as your last resort, and apply it according to package directions.

CURBING CUTWORM ATTACKS

Cutworms are 1- to 2-inch caterpillars that live in the soil and cut seedlings and very young transplants off at the soil line, leaving the seedlings lying on the soil. Digging your garden and raking it will expose cutworms to birds, which will eat them with relish. You can also use cutworm collars to keep them away from seedlings if they are a problem in your garden. Cut toilet paper tubes in half or cut the bottom out of small paper cups and push them over your seedlings.

JAPANESE BEETLES: TWO CONTROL TACTICS

Japanese beetles are metallic blue or green beetles, ½ inch long, that chew flowers and leaves. The best way to control the adult beetles is to pay your kids or grandkids to pick them off your flowers by hand and squish them or drop them into a pail of soapy water to drown. Beetle traps can be effective if you place them at least 50 feet away from your flower bed and if you don't attract every beetle in the town-

Hand picking is the easiest nontoxic way to control Japanese beetles. Just drop them into a jar or can of soapy water.

ship with the pheromone lures that come with most beetle traps.

Controlling Japanese beetles by controlling their grubs, which eat the roots of lawn grasses and other plants, is only possible if you can get everyone in your neighborhood involved. If everyone applies milky disease spores to their lawns, you will see a reduction in beetle populations after a year or so. If you have serious infestations and your flowers are at stake, pyrethrum is very effective. Spray it according to package directions.

SLUGS AND SNAILS: COOL CONTROLS

Unfortunately, slugs and snails are attracted to gardens covered with natural organic mulch. They love cool, moist soil and will hide in it during the day. They come out at night to rasp holes in leaves in your garden—flowers, too, if they are close enough to the soil. You can catch slugs and snails in traps like the ones shown on this page and then dispose of them. Diatomaceous earth is an effective control, too. Sprinkle it around plants that are being attacked. It feels like baby powder to humans but feels more like razor blades to crawling insects, including slugs. You need to reapply it after each rain. Birds and toads will munch on slugs, which is reason enough to welcome them to your garden.

Slugs will fall into shallow containers filled with stale beer and drown. Another way to trap them is to tuck cabbage leaves or grapefruit halves under your flowers. Slugs and snails will take refuge under them during the heat of the day, and you can scrape them out into soapy water.

Stopping Spider Mites

Spider mites are nearly microscopic ($\frac{1}{50}$ of an inch) spiderlike creatures that cluster under leaves and on stem tips. They cover the undersides of leaves and stem tips with fine webbing, too. Spider mites prefer hot, dry conditions, and you can use that knowledge to control them with your hose. Spray infested plants daily with a strong stream of water. Keeping the soil moist discourages them, too. Use insecticidal soap for serious infestations, making sure to spray both sides of the leaves.

Final Thoughts

Soil preparation and a good course of preventive maintenance—watering, mulching, and taking steps to control diseases and pests before they get out of hand—are the easiest ways to have a beautiful garden without spending all your time worrying about problems. If you give your flowers a good start each season, they'll be able to take care of themselves quite effectively, without much assistance from you. That leaves you with plenty of time to pick flowers and enjoy your garden—or perhaps plan another garden for next year!

Spring

It's easy to fall in love with flowers in spring, when they take the barren ground of winter and cover it with color. So spring's where I'll start on our tour of beautiful easy flower gardens. The easiest way to get you excited about creating your own flower garden is to show you some of the possibilities. In the pages that follow, you'll find a host of ideas you can use in your own yard—gorgeous combinations of easy-care flowers, ideas for turning problem sites into colorful gardens, and simple tips for creating your own designs. Let's go!

Virginia bluebells (*Mertensia virginica*) are just one of the many shade-loving wildflowers that are perfect for a site under a tree. Combine them with ferns, hostas, or other shade lovers because they'll disappear after their glorious spring show—only to reappear the following spring.

Here's a spring scene that really *is* as pretty as a picture, and here's why. The owners combined masses of spring-blooming bulbs with a showy spring-flowering dogwood. Tulips and other spring bulbs like the grape hyacinths shown here are most effective when planted in drifts of a dozen or more.

*E*asy-to-grow candytuft (*Iberis sempervirens*) is a carpet of snowy blooms in spring. This sun-loving perennial is appealing used as a groundcover, as an edging for a flower border, or trailing over a wall.

*I*nstead of struggling to grow garden flowers on a soggy site, explore some of the wonderful bog plants that thrive in wet soil. Marsh marigolds (*Caltha palustris*) are a beautiful choice—and as you can see, they don't mind wet feet.

You don't need a rocky site to have a rock garden—a rock wall is perfect! This brilliant spring display includes a variety of mound-forming plants that thrive in well-drained soil: basket-of-gold (*Aurinia saxatilis*), moss phlox (*Phlox subulata*), and wall rock cress (*Arabis caucasica*).

Here's the perfect combination for a sunny cottage garden: pink lupines and white Shasta daisies.

The heady perfume of lilacs can put magic in the air of a late-spring garden. Here's a tip: Use these large shrubs as backdrops for perennials and annuals.

*F*or a sunny, dry site, German chamomile (*Matricaria recutita*) and bright orange California poppies (*Eschscholzia californica*) make a cheerful combination.

*D*affodils, tulips, and hostas are perfect companions. Just as the bulbs finish blooming, the green-and-white–patterned hosta leaves emerge to hide the bulbs' yellowing foliage.

Give your groundcovers a spring facelift by planting spring bulbs in your groundcover bed. Here, periwinkle grows happily with daffodils, grape hyacinths, hyacinths, and tulips.

You can create a beautiful garden under trees by planting a carpet of shade-loving groundcovers like Allegheny foamflower (*Tiarella cordifolia*). Allegheny foamflower is a woodland wildflower with lacy flower spikes in spring.

Old-fashioned pink bleeding-heart (*Dicentra spectabilis*) is a spectacular spring perennial. When its bloom is over, it performs a disappearing act, going dormant until next spring. So to avoid a gap in your garden, combine it with summer-flowering perennials, or plant it with a blooming groundcover like lamium (*Lamium maculatum*), which will fill its space through the summer.

Add a skirt of spring-blooming flowers to a row of azaleas, and you have a very colorful shade garden. This lovely combination features lilies-of-the-valley, blue forget-me-nots, pulmonaria, ajuga, and pink fringed bleeding heart.

Here's a lovely low-growing combination for a wall or rock garden. The blue blooms of Serbian bellflower (*Campanula poscharskyana*) spill over yellow-flowered and variegated sedums and nestle against a clump of variegated sedges (*Carex* spp.).

Daylilies and daisies—what could be easier? If you're choosy about the daylilies you plant, you can have them in bloom from spring to fall. Mix types described as early, midseason, and late blooming for an uninterrupted show.

*I*nvite birds into your garden along with the flowers. Here, a birdbath sets off this lovely spring display of rosy columbines and pink astilbes. Don't forget that columbines are at the top of hummingbirds' list of spring favorites.

Wouldn't you love a gorgeous spring garden like this? Well, guess what—you can have it. All of these perennials are as easy to grow as they are beautiful. These two borders feature a pink, blue, and white color scheme using clumps of foxgloves, Siberian iris, peonies, and other flowers.

For an eye-level burst of color, train roses to climb over an arbor. Once you have your arbor, it's easy to create a rose-covered sitting area you will enjoy again and again. Just nestle a garden bench in the shade under the arbor.

Here's the secret to creating gardens that look attractive all season long: plants with colorful, long-lasting foliage. These hostas, sedums, and 'Palace Purple' heuchera are just three possibilities.

*T*his beautiful easy garden of daylilies, purple Canterbury bells, and foxgloves is protected by a low, unobtrusive fence made of chicken wire. While a low fence won't deter large animal pests like deer, it is quite effective at keeping rabbits from sampling your flowers.

Primroses add beautiful spring color to a damp site. Use all one shade, or combine different cultivars for a blaze of color.

Cranesbills (*Geranium* spp.), also known as hardy geraniums, are among the easiest, most reliable perennials you can grow. They form mound-shaped plants that are covered with showy pink, blue, violet, rose, or white blooms in spring and summer.

There's nothing like a white picket fence to set off old-fashioned favorites like sweet William (*Dianthus barbatus*) and foxglove (*Digitalis purpureus*). Both of these cottage-garden flowers will self-sow generously, providing seedlings you can move to other parts of the garden.

If you use my beautiful easy gardening techniques instead of spraying your garden with chemicals, your flower garden will be alive with beneficial insects like this lady beetle. They will work hard to help keep pest insects in check.

Lavender-pink cranesbills and the frothy, yellow-green flowers of lady's mantle (*Alchemilla mollis*) make appealing bedfellows in a lightly shaded site.

Repeating flower colors and shapes throughout your garden is an easy, effective way to create an attractive design. The repetition of spiky shapes and low mounds carries your eye along this border, and the purple and pink color scheme makes all these plants work well together.

Everybody knows delphiniums are beautiful, but they're also easy if you grow them where summers don't get too hot. If you're a New England or West Coast gardener, your delphiniums will rival the best in Britain.

Yes, you *can* have a beautiful easy rose garden! To create one, plant a selection of the new disease-resistant roses that are as tough as they are beautiful.

Shade doesn't have to be dark and dingy. White- or yellow-marked leaves can light up shade gardens on even the darkest days. This shade-loving planting features variegated hostas and 'Beacon Silver' lamium, as well as colorful impatiens.

Planting in bold clumps of three to five of each kind of plant makes your garden fill in fast and really shows off the flowers you've chosen. This colorful spring display features pinks, white and blue Siberian iris, blue catmint, foxgloves, and peonies.

A picket fence provides the perfect backdrop for a perennial border that's just bursting with blooming foxgloves, pale pink cranesbills, and purple salvias. In this case, the flowers are decorating a fence that encloses a vegetable garden.

Oxeye daisies (*Chrysanthemum leucanthemum*) and purple clustered bellflowers (*Campanula glomerata*) make colorful companions in a sunny site. Cutting the plants back close to the ground after they flower will neaten them up and encourage them to bloom again later in the summer.

*C*heck out local plant sales held by garden clubs or public gardens for easy-care perennials to add to your yard. You are likely to find old favorites like sundrops (*Oenothera* spp.) at bargain prices.

*F*or color that lasts and lasts, mix annuals, perennials, and bulbs in your beautiful easy garden. In this garden, you'll find lilies plus annuals like snapdragons, zinnias, nasturtiums, marigolds, and purple larkspur.

*T*o get the most enjoyment out of your roses, plant groundcovers or herbs like lavender or catmint under them for a beautiful, fragrant display.

Perennial flax (*Linum perenne*) produces silky, lavender-blue flowers for weeks. Its delicate fernlike blue-green leaves belie its sturdy nature: It forms long-lived clumps and thrives in well-drained, dry soil in full sun.

Mass plantings are a simple way to make a beautiful, bold garden. Here, masses of pink astilbe, ferns, and lady's mantle create a dramatic show with the white hydrangea clusters.

Many herbs are every bit as pretty as flowers—and they're generally easy to grow. Here, feverfew (generally considered an herb) and foxglove make a happy combination. Thyme, lavender, yarrow, and purple fennel are other herbs that are at home in both herb and perennial gardens.

Sometimes a packet of seed is all it takes to make a colorful planting. A planting of cornflowers like this one can be sown right in the garden and requires little care once the seeds are up and growing.

Nothing beats a planting of annuals for instant garden color and gratification. In this beautiful easy annual garden, edgings of silver-leaved dusty miller mixed with snowy white sweet alyssum contain a river of color. A mix of marigolds, pansies, and blue violas brighten the center of the bed.

*I*n a shade garden, foliage can be as important as flowers. This elegant planting features ferns, including the lovely, silver-splashed Japanese painted fern, purple-leaved ajuga, glossy European wild ginger, and a few white blooms from ferny-leaved fringed bleeding heart.

Peonies will bloom for 50 years or more in your garden, so take the time to compare flower forms and colors and plant the ones that really appeal to you.

You don't have to like orange to love oriental poppies. You can now buy cultivars with red, white, purple, or bicolored blooms, or add a soft pastel touch with pink poppies like these.

Dress up your rustic fence with a splash of red roses. Roses are perfect "peek-through" flowers for a fence, giving your neighbors as much pleasure as they give you. Maybe you'll start a trend in your neighborhood!

Designs for Beautiful Easy Gardens

The 11 beautiful easy garden
designs in this section will provide
plenty of ideas and inspiration
to keep your garden growing
more beautiful every year.

Beautiful Easy Perennials

An Easy Classic Border

IT MAY COME AS A SURPRISE, but perennial borders don't have to be maintenance hogs. They also don't have to contain 60 or 80 different hard-to-grow plants in order to be effective. What they do need is great plants, like the ones featured in this garden. All are garden classics: They multiply from year to year, have long-lasting blooms, and are easy to grow. The design also features flowers for all seasons — from early spring crocuses to hardy mums and 'Autumn Joy' sedum for fall.

This border is perfect if you're just getting into perennials or if you've grown a few perennials but never tried a whole garden of them.

6' × 20'

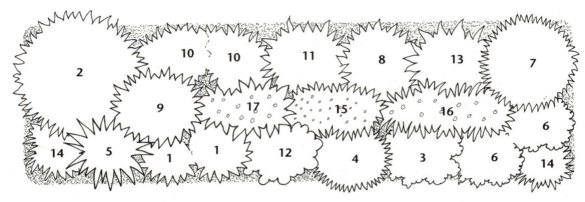

1. Bearded irises
2. Butterfly bush
3. Columbines
4. Coreopsis
5. Daylily
6. Garden mums
7. Gayfeather
8. Orange coneflower
9. Peony

10. Phlox
11. Purple coneflower
12. Sedum 'Autumn Joy'
13. Shasta daisy
14. Sweet Williams
15. Crocuses
16. Daffodils
17. Tulips

You'll have colorful flowers all year with this beautiful easy perennial garden.

PLANTS TO BUY

Buy one of each of the following perennials, unless otherwise noted:

- Bearded irises. Buy two.
- Butterfly bush
- Columbines. Buy three.
- Coreopsis
- Daylily
- Garden mums. Buy two.
- Gayfeather
- Orange coneflower
- Peony
- Phlox. Buy two.
- Purple coneflower
- Sedum 'Autumn Joy'
- Shasta daisy
- Sweet Williams. Buy two or three.

BULBS TO BUY

Buy a dozen of each of the following bulbs, unless otherwise noted:

- Crocuses. Buy a dozen or two.
- Daffodils
- Tulips

THE PLANT GUIDE

PLANTS FOR A BEAUTIFUL EASY PERENNIAL BORDER

THIS garden features plants that need a sunny spot to grow and bloom well. Early-spring bloomers include crocuses, daffodils, tulips, and columbines. Bearded irises, peonies, and Shasta daisies follow from late spring to early summer. During the height of summer, coreopsis, daylilies, gayfeathers, orange and purple coneflowers, phlox, and sweet Williams fill the border with color. Fall features flowers of butterfly bush, hardy mums, and sedum 'Autumn Joy' until the first hard frost ends the season.

Many of these flowers come in a wide range of colors, and I've left the choice up to you. Pick colors you like, but when you pick, consider what other flowers will be in bloom at the same time. For example, if you don't like the sight of orange next to hot pink, pick your daylilies and phlox accordingly—soft yellow or peach daylilies might work better with pink phlox. Or pick white phlox to go with orange daylilies and coneflowers.

Plants

Buy one of each of the following perennials, unless otherwise noted:

Bearded irises (*Iris* hybrids). Look for tall bearded irises for this garden; they're sometimes sold as *I. germanica*. They bloom in late spring and come in nearly every color you can imagine, from solid colors in pastel pinks and blues to brilliant yellows, purples, and pinks, and range in height from 6 to 30 inches. Two-tone blooms are also available. Buy two plants of whatever colors appeal to you. Zones 4 to 9.

Butterfly bush (*Buddleia davidii*). Orange-eye butterfly bush is such a large, bushy plant that it is often treated as a shrub, even though the plant dies back to the ground each winter. Plants reach up to 4 feet tall and wide. The blooms, which appear from midsummer until frost, look like small lilacs; they even come in some of the same colors—lavender, red violet, and purple. They attract butterflies like magnets. Zones 5 to 9.

Columbine (*Aquilegia* × *hybrida*). There are dozens of hybrid columbines to choose from. Colors range from solid purple to white, plus two-tone combinations in everything from red and yellow to violet and white. The flowers, which are held above attractive ferny blue-green foliage, appear in May or June. For this garden, look for a hybrid that's about 3 feet tall, such as one of the McKana strain cultivars. Buy three plants to form a cluster. Zones 3 to 9.

Coreopsis (*Coreopsis* spp.). Also called tickseeds, these summer-blooming perennials bear daisylike flowers in pale to brilliant yellow as well as pale pink. They're generally 1 to 2 feet tall, although threadleaf coreopsis can reach 3 feet. Some cultivars to look for are *C. grandiflora* 'Early Sunrise', *C. lanceolata* 'Sunburst' and 'Sunray', and *C. verticillata* 'Golden Showers' or 'Zagreb'. Zones 3 to 9, depending on the species and cultivars you select.

Daylilies (*Hemerocallis* spp.). Daylilies are among the easiest and most rewarding perennials you can grow. One plant will produce a clump 2 to 3 feet across in a couple of years and produce an endless parade of flowers for weeks in the summer. Flowers come in yellow, orange, pink, maroon, and nearly white. Buy any color you like. Zones 2 to 9.

Garden mum (*Chrysanthemum* × *morifolium*, also sold as *Dendranthema* × *grandiflorum*). Even nongardeners recognize garden mums. They're a sure sign of fall, but these days, you can also buy forced plants in spring and get two seasons of color out of them—the first year at least. They'll revert to fall-only blooming in your garden. Colors range from white through pink, rose, red, burgundy, gold, yellow, and cream, and the plants vary in size from 1½ to 5 feet tall. The style of the flower heads varies considerably and can be button, pompon, daisy, or spider. For this garden, buy two plants of whatever bloom color or type you like. Be sure to buy garden mums, though, and not one of the potted florist mums sold for indoor gift plants. Florist mums will survive from year to year but generally won't manage to flower in the garden before frost destroys the blooms. Zones 4 to 9.

Gayfeathers (*Liatris* spp.). Also called blazing-stars, these natives of

Phlox

Purple coneflower

Orange coneflower

Gayfeather

Shasta daisy

This garden features an especially nice selection of flowers for cutting. Once the garden is established, you'll have flowers for arrangements from spring to frost.

the American prairie produce fuzzy-looking spikes of densely packed flowers in mauve, violet, pale purple, and red violet. Strangely enough, the flowers on the spikes open from the top down. Depending on the species

you pick, plants can range from 1 to 5 feet tall—2 to 3 feet is about average. Blooms appear in mid- to late summer. Zones 3 or 4 to 9.

Orange coneflower (*Rudbeckia fulgida*). Also known as brown-eyed Susans, the golden orange petals and chocolate brown centers of these easy-to-grow summer daisies decorate this border for nearly a month in mid- to late summer. Orange coneflowers are 2 to 3 feet tall and will spread. 'Goldsturm' is an outstanding cultivar. Zones 3 to 9.

Peony (*Paeonia lactiflora*). What garden should be without a clump of glorious, late-spring–blooming peonies? Peonies are generally available for sale in the fall and are sold bareroot. Although you may see potted peonies for sale, you'll get the most for your money if you buy three- to five-eye (bud) bareroot divisions. Healthy, three- to five-eye divisions will bloom sooner than smaller, one- or two-eye ones, which are sometimes potted up for sale. There are peonies with single and double blooms, and they come in luscious shades of pink, white, and red. Peonies grow from 1½ to 3 feet tall. Look around and buy one plant that appeals to you. Zones 3 to 8.

Phlox (*Phlox paniculata*). Garden phlox is a classic, summer-blooming perennial that's a must for this garden. Plants bear domed clusters of white, pink, or magenta flowers on 2- to 3-foot plants. Look for mildew-resistant cultivars, including 'Bright Eyes', 'David', 'Eva Cullum', and 'Franz Schubert'. Or try cultivars of thick leaf phlox (*P. carolina*), which are very mildew-resistant. Look for 'Miss Lingard', 'Omega', or 'Rosalinde'. Buy two plants. Zones 3 or 4 to 9, depending on the species and cultivars you choose.

Purple coneflower (*Echinacea purpurea*). The daisylike blooms of this native American wildflower sport a surprising combination of colors — purplish pink petals with orange-brown centers. White-flowered cultivars are also available. Both types bloom from July until frost and reach 2 to 4 feet. Zones 3 to 8.

'Autumn Joy' sedum (*Sedum* 'Autumn Joy'). In the fall, the flowers of this classic succulent perennial are covered with butterflies and bees. Plants form attractive 2-foot mounds that have all-season interest. They have fleshy green leaves, followed by flat-topped clusters of green flower buds that resemble broccoli until they turn pink and then bronze in the fall. The dried flowers will stand in the garden until you remove them in late winter — they're also great for dried arrangements. Zones 3 to 9.

Shasta daisy (*Chrysanthemum* × *superbum*, also sold as *Leucanthemum* × *superbum*). This beloved garden perennial bears white-petaled daisies with gold button centers in early summer. Plants range from 1 to 3 feet tall. For this garden, look for one of the taller types — 'Aglaya', 'Alaska', and 'Mount Shasta' are all good choices. Zones 4 to 8; 'Alaska' is hardy to Zone 3.

Sweet William (*Dianthus barbatus*). Hardy, old-fashioned sweet William is actually a biennial, but since it self-sows freely, it behaves like a perennial. Plants produce dense round heads of bicolored flowers in pink, red, and white from spring into summer and reach 10 to 18 inches in height. This plant is easy to grow from seed, too. Buy two or three plants. Zones 3 to 9.

Bulbs

Bulbs are offered for sale from late summer to fall, which is also the right time to plant them. You can look over the display at your local nursery, or buy from one of the colorful catalogs that arrive in your mailbox.

Crocuses (*Crocus* spp.). One of the earliest harbingers of spring, crocuses often push right up through the snow. Buy a dozen or two so that next year they can remind you that spring is on its way. Zones 3 to 9.

Daffodils (*Narcissus* spp.). There are hundreds of daffodils to choose from. Look at your local garden center or in mail-order catalogs and pick your favorites. When you buy daffodils, spend a little more to get the larger, better-quality bulbs rather than the super-cheap assortments — trust me, it's worth it. For more on buying quality bulbs, see the illustration on page 167. Buy a dozen bulbs. Zones 4 to 9, depending on the species and cultivars you select.

Tulips (*Tulipa* spp.). You'll find tulips displayed right next to the daffodils in your local garden center or listed near them in your favorite catalog. Buy a dozen bulbs of any color or colors you like. Unlike daffodils, tulips generally don't multiply from year to year. In fact, they tend to peter out and need replacing every few years. Darwin hybrid tulips, single late tulips, and many species tulips are generally long-lived and dependable, though. Zones 5 to 8.

THE SEASONAL GUIDE

SEASON ONE
(JANUARY AND FEBRUARY)

Select a Site

Late winter can be a frustrating time for gardeners. It's too early to work the soil but not too early to dream about getting out and getting your hands dirty. Use some of your excess energy looking for the perfect site for this garden.

The main requirement is a site that receives at least six full hours of golden sunshine. Since this is a border, it is a rather long, thin design — approximately 6 feet wide and 20 feet long. You could plant it next to a garage or house, along a fence, or next to a walkway. You'll enjoy it anywhere in your yard where you want glorious flowers.

Buy Plants and Supplies

You probably can buy all of the plants for this garden at local gardens and nurseries once spring gets rolling and displays of perennials are stocked up. But it's fun to order by mail, too, and it can be more economical. For a list of mail-order companies that sell perennials, see "Where to Buy" on this page.

Most of the plants in this garden can be planted in late spring or early summer, but as you get ready for planting, keep in mind that your peony and the hardy bulbs (crocuses, tulips, and daffodils) are planted in fall.

In addition to the plants listed for this garden, you'll need the following supplies:

- Four 40-pound bags of compost or composted manure. Or substitute homemade compost — one full bin or three wheelbarrows full.

- Two 4-cubic-foot bags of more organic matter such as compost, chopped leaves, or rotted sawdust

- One 5-pound bag of natural organic fertilizer

- One 50-foot soaker hose, ¾ inch in diameter

- Six large bags of shredded organic mulch, such as pine bark, cedar bark, or pine needles. Or sub-

WHERE TO BUY

All of the perennials in this garden will be easy to find at your local garden center or nursery. Or you can order them from one of the catalogs listed in "Where to Buy" on page 155. If you don't mind starting with smaller plants, you can save money by ordering from one of the catalogs listed here.

- Bluestone Perennials, 7211 Middle Ridge Road, Madison, OH 44057

- W. Atlee Burpee & Co., 300 Park Avenue, Warminster, PA 18974

- Henry Field's Seed & Nursery Co., 415 North Burnett, Shenandoah, IA 51602

- Gurney's Seed & Nursery Co., 110 Capital Street, Yankton, SD 57079

- Milaeger's Gardens, 4838 Douglas Avenue, Racine, WI 53402-2498

- Spring Hill Nurseries, 6523 North Galena Road, Peoria, IL 61656

stitute an equivalent amount of your own compost or a mix of compost and shredded leaves.

SEASON TWO
(MARCH, APRIL, AND MAY)

Prepare the Site

You have two options for preparing the site and planting this garden. You can prepare the soil and plant everything but your peony and hardy bulbs in early to mid-spring, as soon as the ground can be easily worked with a rotary tiller or garden spade. Or you can improve the soil during the summer, and plant the garden in September. See "Getting Your Garden Ready to Plant" on page 42 for complete information on preparing the soil.

To prepare for late spring or early summer planting, select a day when the soil is warm and there is not much prospect for a late spring frost. First, mark off your site with short stakes so you don't lose track of its dimensions. Then clear away any rocks and debris. Use a sharp garden spade to remove any grass that is growing there. Use the grass you've spaded up to patch spots in your lawn, or place it upside down on your compost pile.

All of the plants in this garden prefer soil with a neutral pH (near 7.0). Have your soil pH tested through your local Cooperative Extension Service office (listed under city or county governments in your telephone book), or buy a home-test kit and do it yourself. Then spread compost or composted manure, other organic matter like shredded leaves, natural organic fertilizer, and lime (if recommended by your soil test results) evenly over the entire site. To incorporate all the soil amendments and make

the soil as crumbly and smooth as possible, till the soil with a rotary tiller or garden spade to a depth of 8 inches. Rake the area smooth, and you're ready to plant.

Plant the Garden

Try to plant this garden on a cloudy, overcast day to minimize stress for the plants. If you can't wait for a cloudy day, at least plant everything late in the day to minimize the sun's harsh effects.

When you are ready to put in your perennial border, start by arranging your plants in the spots where you want to plant them. To follow my garden design on page 94, start at the back left of the border and draw a 5-foot-diameter circle in the soil with a stick, trowel, or other tool. Place the butterfly bush in the center of the circle. Next to the site for the butterfly bush, draw an oval-shaped planting area that's about 5 feet long and 2 feet wide, and place the two phlox plants at either end. Continue drawing circles along the back of the border— each about 2½ feet in diameter—for the purple coneflower, orange coneflower, Shasta daisy, and gayfeather.

Before you start drawing circles and reserving space for the plants that will fill in the front of the border, draw a 3-foot circle in front of the phlox and to the right of the butterfly bush to reserve space for the peony that you'll be planting in fall. As you can see from the design on page 94, most of the rest of the middle row is reserved for hardy bulbs, which you'll also plant in early fall.

Start the front row with an oval-shaped planting area for the sweet William, which will fill in around the base of the butterfly bush. (You may have room for two plants of sweet William on this end of the border.) Then continue down the front of the border, drawing circles and placing plants, as shown on the design on page 94. All the plants get between 2½ and 3 feet of space except the tall bearded irises. Allow for a site that's about 2 feet wide and 4 feet long for them.

Before you plant anything, step back and look at the garden from several angles to see if you like the arrangement. Then, starting at the back of the garden, plant each plant in the site you've selected by digging a hole large enough to hold the root ball. (If you have bareroot plants, make sure there's enough room to spread the roots out in the hole.) Make each hole only deep enough so the crown of the plant, the point where the top of the plant meets the roots, is at ground level. To refill

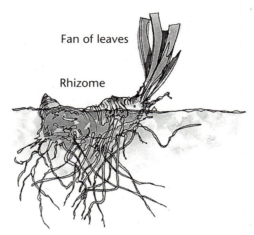

Fan of leaves

Rhizome

Tall bearded irises grow from a fleshy rhizome that creeps along the soil surface. When planting, be sure the top of the rhizome is above the soil surface. Otherwise, it may rot.

the hole, distribute the soil around the plant and press down firmly with your hands. Water thoroughly.

The tall bearded irises need to be planted somewhat differently than the rest of the plants in this garden. They have fleshy rhizomes, which are actually creeping stems. They look a lot like the fresh ginger you can buy in the produce section of the grocery store, although they usually have a short fan of leaves attached when you buy them. The important thing to remember when you plant irises is that you don't want to bury the rhizome underground. Instead, you want to plant it so that its top side is exposed.

To plant the irises, space one at either end of their planting site, 1 foot in from each end and 2 feet from each other. Dig a shallow trench for each rhizome and place it with the fan of leaves facing upward. Cover it with soil and press down firmly. Then carefully remove some of the soil on top of the rhizome to expose the upper part—just enough so you can see it. Water the irises well.

The hard part is over now. Your perennial border is planted! Since your perennials will be small the first year—it may take them a season or two to fill in—you may want to plant annuals between them for extra color at first. Any of the annuals in the "Beautiful Easy Annuals" garden on page 107 would make fine fillers.

The last step in the planting process is to mulch your garden. But before you do, snake your soaker hose through the garden in a sort of S-curve, covering as much of the garden as possible. Be sure to leave the connecting end visible so you can find it.

Then cover the entire garden and the soaker hose with a 2- to 4-inch-thick layer of a natural organic mulch, such as shredded bark. Natural organic mulch, as opposed to synthetic landscape fabric or weed mats, is essential for the health and well-being of this garden. Since it is a perennial garden, you won't till the soil each year to add extra organic matter. Instead, the mulch you put down is going to decompose over the course of the season and add organic matter to the garden for you.

SEASON THREE (JUNE, JULY, AND AUGUST)

Minimize Chores and Enjoy Your Garden

There is a very good chance this garden will not need a lot of water. The mulch you added at planting time will hold moisture in the soil and keep it cool and moist. Mulch also suppresses weeds so it saves you watering and weeding time. When you do need to water, attach your regular garden hose to the soaker hose, then turn on the water and let it run for one to two hours, or until the soil in the garden is soaked to a depth of 6 inches. Don't water any more than once a week, but be sure to water thoroughly when you do.

Phlox is the only flower in this garden that may be attacked by a disease or pest—it is often attacked by powdery mildew. Powdery mildew causes white or gray spots on the leaves, and afflicted leaves eventually turn yellow and drop off.

The best defense against powdery mildew is to plant resistant cultivars, and be sure to keep your phlox in full sun with plenty of good air circulation and not too much dampness in the soil. Thinning out the clumps by removing some of the stems at the base of the plant improves air circulation. In fall, cut the plants down and throw away the stems to discourage mildew from overwintering in your garden.

SEASON FOUR (SEPTEMBER AND OCTOBER)

Plant the Peony and Bulbs

September and early October are the best times of the year to plant crocus, daffodil, and tulip bulbs as well as peonies. To plant your peony, find the spot in the back left of the garden that you reserved for it. You want to plant your divisions so the roots can spread out, so dig a hole wide enough and deep enough to comfortably accommodate them. Be sure the pink eyes on the roots will be no more than 2 inches below the soil surface when your peony is finally settled in the soil. Peonies that are planted too deep won't bloom, so after you cover the roots with soil, double-check the depth of the buds. Then gently tamp down the site, and water well.

To plant the bulbs, place them on the soil surface in little clusters of two or three across the center of the garden. This creates a more natural look than planting in one long straight line. Using a trowel or specialized bulb planter, dig holes 10 inches deep for the daffodils, 8 inches deep for the tulips, and 4 inches deep for the crocuses. Place a bulb in each hole, pointed end up. (If you're not sure which way to plant, look for signs of roots.) Fill the hole with soil and press down firmly.

Next spring, after your hardy bulbs have bloomed, don't cut their tops off. You can cut off any flower stems, but you must leave the leaves until they turn brown because they are making food and flowers for next

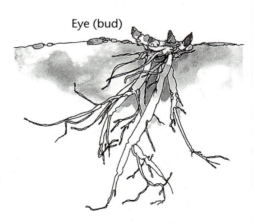

Eye (bud)

One common peony problem is easy to prevent: Don't plant the clumps too deeply or they won't bloom.

season's display. Once the leaves turn brown in midsummer, you can cut them off and compost them. Or just leave them where they are and they'll add organic matter to the soil without any help from you.

You can sprinkle a handful of natural organic fertilizer or bonemeal on top of the soil over the bulbs and toss a shovelful of compost over that. This gives the bulbs extra food to store up during late summer and early fall.

Prepare the Garden for Winter

Fall can be a rather dry time of the year, and nothing kills expensive new perennials like dry weather. Be sure to keep up your watering through Halloween, skipping it once in a while if you receive a good rain.

The hardy mums, orange coneflower, and 'Autumn Joy' sedum will continue blooming through several light frosts. As the other plants are hit with frost and begin to brown, remove their stems and toss them in the compost bin. Once the cold weather really arrives, cut all of the plants down to 1 to 2 inches above the soil line. Remove the soaker hose, drain it, and store it for the winter.

When the ground is frozen, cover the garden with a 2- to 3-inch layer of shredded leaves, compost, or a com-bination of the two to protect the garden from winter's cold. A blanket of heavy snow is the best protection, but a warm winter, full of freezing and thawing, can push perennials up out of the ground where they can be damaged by the cold. Winter mulch will protect your garden like a blanket. In a pinch, evergreen boughs cut from the Christmas tree offer great protection, too.

Now all you need to do is wait until next spring to watch your perennial border repeat the process. You'll have a better display of flowers each year!

Chances are, you won't need to dig and divide your thriving perennials until their third year in the garden—even later in the case of the daylily, sedum, and daffodils. You won't need to divide your peony for many years and can leave the butterfly bush alone as well.

Fall is the very best time to dig up, separate, and replant perennials. When that time comes, dig up the entire plant, gently pull the root ball apart so you are left with two or three smaller plants rather than one big one. You must dig and divide most of the perennials in this garden every three or four years, or the center of the clumps will die and the plants will lose vigor and decline.

Beautiful Easy Annuals

Bold Flowers
for Summer Color

THE FIRST FLOWERS *I can remember planting were marigolds and zinnias in my mother's garden. I've loved annuals ever since. They're easy to grow and will bloom their heads off with just a little care. Most common varieties are available in a range of colors; it's fun to try new combinations every year.*

Some people may think this garden is just too easy, but it will provide you with a summer-long supply of color and plenty of spectacular flowers to bring indoors for bouquets as well. Growing annuals is also a good way for beginners to learn what it takes to grow flowers. If you're a more experienced gardener, grow this garden to bring back old memories — or to share your love of flowers with a child.

6′ × 15′

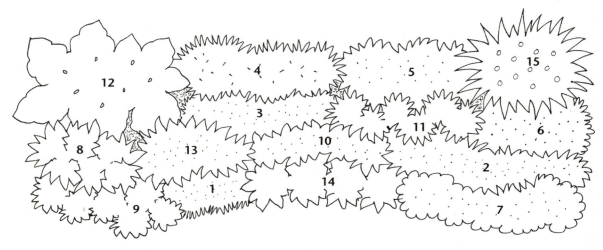

1. California poppies
2. China asters
3. Cornflowers
4. Cosmos
5. Four-o'clocks
6. Marigolds
7. Nasturtiums
8. Nicotianas
9. Petunias
10. Pot marigolds
11. Snapdragons
12. Sunflowers
13. Zinnias
14. Dahlias
15. Glads

SEEDS TO BUY

Buy one packet of each of the following annuals:

- California poppies
- China asters
- Cornflowers
- Cosmos
- Four-o'clocks
- Marigolds
- Nasturtiums
- Pot marigolds
- Sunflowers
- Zinnias

It's hard to beat this garden for nonstop summer color. Cheerful, easy-care annuals add a lot of impact for a little money.

BULBS TO BUY

Buy a dozen tubers or corms of each of the following:

- Dahlias
- Glads

PLANTS TO BUY

Buy a "six-pack" of each of the following annuals:

- Nicotiana
- Petunias
- Snapdragons

THE PLANT GUIDE

ANNUALS FOR A BEAUTIFUL EASY GARDEN

THIS IS A GARDEN that's at its best during high summer. It features a mix of annuals, including some of the new sunflowers developed to use as cut flowers, old-fashioned four-o'clocks and bachelor's-buttons, as well as a cluster of glads for beautiful bouquets. All of the flowers in this garden will bloom all summer long and thrive in full sun.

Seeds

Buy one packet of each of the following annuals:

California poppies (*Eschscholzia californica*). These California natives produce showy, 3-inch, cup-shaped flowers in brilliant orange or yellow. They make wonderful plants for the front of a border because they only grow 10 inches tall and bloom from summer to fall. They'll self-sow, too.

China asters (*Callistephus chinensis*). Also called annual asters, these plants in the daisy family are available with daisylike or fully double flowers. They come in purple, crimson, lavender, pink, and white. Flowers range in size from 2 to 5 inches across. For this garden, select any flower color or type you like, but look for plants that are medium-tall—maturing at 2 to 2½ feet.

Cornflowers (*Centaurea cyanus*). These fragrant, old-fashioned flowers are also known as bachelor's-buttons. Their 1- to 1½-inch flowers come in blue, maroon, pink, lavender, and white. Buy a packet of seeds of mixed colors or a single color that appeals to you. Don't buy dwarf plants for this garden, though; look for plants that grow about 2 feet tall.

Cosmos (*Cosmos* spp.). One of the easiest of all annuals to grow, cosmos bears daisylike flowers in many different colors. Garden cosmos

(*C. bipinnatus*) has crimson, pink, and white flowers; yellow cosmos (*C. sulphureus*) bears gold, golden orange, and orange-scarlet flowers. For this garden, look for taller types that reach 3 or 4 feet at least. Cultivars to look for include 'Picotee', which has white petals edged in pink, 'Bright Lights', which has red flowers, or the Sensation series cultivars, which come in red, pink, and white. If you like, you can try a new one every year.

Four-o'clocks (*Mirabilis jalapa*). These easy-to-grow, bushy, 3-foot plants produce fragrant, 1-inch blossoms that open at about four o'clock on warm summer afternoons. They bloom from July until frost. You can choose from a range of flower colors, including white, red, pink, yellow, and striped.

Marigolds (*Tagetes* spp.). Open your favorite seed catalog, and you'll see marigolds in all shapes and sizes. Colors include yellow, orange, maroon, and nearly white, and bloom sizes range from 1-inch buttons to flower heads 4 or 5 inches across. Pick a flower size and color you like, but for this garden, look for seeds that will produce 2½- to 3-foot plants.

Nasturtiums (*Tropaeolum majus*). These colorful annuals tolerate drought and poor soil, yet cover themselves with colorful red, orange,

These annuals are great for cutting.

and yellow blooms all summer. The round, shield-shaped leaves, flower buds, and flowers are peppery-tasting and great when added to salads. For this garden, buy a packet of either 'Alaska', which has green leaves variegated with white, or seeds in the Jewel series. Both grow 8 to 12 inches tall.

Pot marigolds (*Calendula officinalis*). Also simply known as calendulas, these popular plants produce double, 2- to 3-inch flowers in yellow, gold, and orange. You'll find many cultivars offered. For this garden, select one that is 12 to 18 inches tall when mature. The flowers are edible and make a nice addition to salads.

Sunflowers (*Helianthus annuus*). Plant breeders have developed many terrific ornamental sunflowers that make great cutting and border plants. Flowers come in lemon, gold, orange, mahogany, or white. For this garden, look for cultivars that reach 3 to 5 feet when mature. Some good ones to look for include creamy yellow 'Italian White', lemon yellow 'Valentine', or maroon and gold 'Velvet Tapestry'.

Zinnias (*Zinnia elegans*). You can't beat common zinnias for summer-long color and flowers for cutting. That is, as long as they receive plenty of sun. For this garden, I suggest you look for mildew-resistant cultivars that are about 2½ feet tall. Try either Burpee's Zenith Hybrid series, which have double, 6-inch blooms in red, orange, yellow, and pink, or Ruffles Hybrid types, which bear 3- to 3½-inch flowers in the same colors. Select any color you like or plant a mix.

Plants

Buy a "six-pack" of each of the annuals listed below. Plants that aren't in bloom yet or are just beginning to show color are your best buy. They won't be as affected by transplant stress as plants in full bloom.

Nicotiana (*Nicotiana alata*). Once you've grown nicotiana, or flowering tobacco, you'll never want to spend a summer without it. These easy, carefree plants bear tube-shaped flowers in red, pink, white, and lime green. If you buy cultivars with white or green flowers, they'll be fragrant at night. For this garden, buy plants of any color or a mix of colors that will be 2 to 2½ feet tall when mature. (The taller types tend to be more fragrant than the dwarf ones.) Southern gardeners with a very early spring could easily grow this plant from seed.

Petunias (*Petunia × hybrida*). Common garden petunias are deservedly popular annuals that cover themselves with flowers throughout the summer. You can find petunias that look like carnations or fancy geraniums in many different colors and patterns. Plants grow 8 to 18 inches tall and wide, with 1½- to 4-inch blooms. For summer-long bloom in warm areas, look for heat-tolerant types like cultivars in the Madness series.

Snapdragons (*Antirrhinum majus*). Common snapdragons bear dense spikes of maroon, pink, yellow, and white flowers that snap open and shut like a dragon's jaws when squeezed from the sides. For this garden, buy snapdragons that will reach 3 feet tall. Plant them early and you will get great flowers all the way to frost.

Bulbs

This garden features two annuals—dahlias and glads—grown from bulb-like structures called corms and tubers.

Dahlias (*Dahlia* spp.). This garden calls for dwarf dahlias that reach only 8 to 12 inches. You can grow these from seed, but for fastest results, look for plants at your local garden center. (Burpee offers plants of 8-inch 'Royal Dahliettas' by mail in a mix of red, orange, yellow, lavender, and white.) Dwarf dahlias will produce tuberous roots you can dig up at the end of the season and store over winter. Buy four plants.

Glads (*Gladiolus* spp.). Gladioli, or glads, grow from small corms, producing strap-shaped leaves and a 3-foot spike that's covered with ruffled flowers that open over several weeks. Plants come in many colors, including maroon, red, lavender, yellow, and white. I've had good luck with inexpensive assortments and expensive singles. Buy a dozen corms.

THE SEASONAL GUIDE

SEASON ONE (JANUARY AND FEBRUARY)

Select a Site

This garden needs a site in full sun. That means the flowers in it need at least six hours of direct sunshine each day. You can make it any shape you like, but the plan I've drawn is about 6 feet wide and 15 feet long. An eastern or southern exposure along a house or fence is good. This bed would look pretty along the edge of your yard, too.

Buy the Seeds, Plants, Bulbs, and Supplies

Have some fun when you select the seeds, plants, and bulbs for your beautiful easy annual garden. You will have lots of colors to choose from. If you love to bring flowers indoors, look for ones that will look pretty with the colors in your home. Or if you simply want to plant a garden that says "Look at me!" buy the brightest colors you can find. Either way, you'll love your beautiful easy annuals.

You should be able to buy all the plants you need for this garden at local garden centers in late spring, but it's fun to order from catalogs, too. See "Where to Buy" on this page for some suggestions of companies to order from. If you would like to plant specific flower colors—pink and yellow to go with your home's decor, for example—be sure to take a look at catalog offerings. In many cases local seed racks only offer packets of mixed-color seeds—'Peter Pan Mix' zinnias, for example. But by mail you can often buy specific colors. Several seed catalogs offer packets of individual colors of 'Peter Pan' zinnias as well as a mix.

In addition to the seeds, plants, and bulbs, you'll need the following supplies:

• Three 40-pound bags of compost or composted manure. Or substitute homemade compost—one full bin or three wheelbarrows full.

• One 5-pound bag of natural organic fertilizer

• One 25-foot soaker hose, 3/4 inch in diameter

• Four to six large bags of shredded organic mulch, such as pine bark, cedar bark, or pine needles. Or substitute an equivalent amount of your own compost or a mix of compost and shredded leaves.

WHERE TO BUY

All of these seeds, plants, and bulbs are readily available at your local garden center. If you would like a special color selection to choose from, write for a catalog from one of the following companies:

• W. Atlee Burpee & Co., 300 Park Avenue, Warminster, PA 18974

• Park Seed Co., Cokesbury Road, Greenwood, SC 29647

• Stokes Seeds, Inc., P.O. Box 548, Buffalo, NY 14240-0548

• Thompson & Morgan, Inc., P.O. Box 1308, Jackson, NJ 08527

SEASON TWO (MARCH, APRIL, AND MAY)

Prepare the Site

Although you can begin to prepare your soil in early spring, you will need to wait until all danger of frost has passed and the soil has warmed up to plant this garden. This could be as early as late February in some southern states and as late as mid-April to May in more northerly climates. Don't try to get too early a start with this garden: Most of these plants would be severely damaged by a late frost.

Before you start preparing your soil, make sure it isn't still too wet and cold to work. See "Getting Your Garden Ready to Plant" on page 42 for complete information on preparing the soil.

When you're ready to prepare your site, first mark off your site with short stakes so you don't lose track of its dimensions, using the garden design on page 108 as a guideline. Then clear away any rocks and debris. Use a sharp spade to remove any grass that is growing there. Use the grass you've removed to patch spots in your lawn or place it upside down on your compost pile.

You'll save yourself effort and aggravation if you can plan ahead and take everything out to the garden site at one time. Carry tools in an empty drywall-compound bucket, and put plants together in a flat. A garden cart or wheelbarrow will let you carry everything you need easily.

Spread the compost or composted manure and natural organic fertilizer evenly over the entire site. To incorporate these soil amendments and make the soil as crumbly and smooth as possible, till the soil with a rotary tiller or garden spade to a depth of 6 to 8 inches. Rake the area smooth, and you are ready to plant.

Plant the Garden

Once your last frost date has come and gone, you can get ready to plant. (If you're not sure when it is, here's a way to guess—it's the time when most of your neighbors plant their tomato plants out in the garden. If you don't want to guess, call your local Cooperative Extension Service office, listed under city or county governments in your phone book.) On a warm dry day, bring all of your seeds, plants, and bulbs out to the garden site.

Use the garden design on page 108 to help you plant your garden. You don't have to follow it exactly if you don't want to, but if you do vary it, just remember to put the taller sunflowers and cosmos in the back, or in the center if you decide on a round or oval design that you can see from all sides. Arrange the rest of the flowers by height, too, with the low-growing plants in the front and along the sides of the garden.

To plant my design, draw four oval circles in the soil with a stick or a trowel along the back of the garden, as shown in the plan. Make the circle largest where you'll be planting the sunflowers, and leave a little bit less space for the other back-row plants. Next, draw long, narrow areas—3 to 4 feet long and about 1 to 1½ feet wide—for the cornflowers, snapdragons, and marigolds. Finally, draw planting areas in the soil for the two front rows of the garden. You don't need to draw squares or circles or ovals—free-form bubble shapes will create a natural effect once they are filled with flowers.

Plant the glads first in the back right-hand corner. Place the 12 corms evenly around in the oval, no closer than 6 inches apart. Dig holes 4 inches deep and place a corm, root side down, in the hole and cover with soil, pressing down with your hands. As the glads grow, you may want to mound some additional soil up around their stems to provide support. Or place unobtrusive wooden stakes near the stems to keep them standing straight.

Next, plant the nicotiana, petunia, and snapdragon plants. Before planting, pinch off all the flowers. This is important because it gives the plants time to sink roots into the soil and become adjusted to their new environment. Once established, they'll begin blooming again and will produce more flowers than plants that weren't pinched at planting time.

After you've pinched off the flowers, space the plants in their circles. Then dig holes with your trowel that are large enough to hold the plants comfortably. Be sure to give their roots plenty of room to spread out. Place the plants in each hole so that the crown, the point where the roots meet the top of the plant, is level with the soil. Refill the holes, gather soil around the plants, and press down firmly with your hands. Water each plant well.

Plant the dahlias next, by digging a hole 4 to 6 inches deep for each plant. If you're putting in plants, treat them the same way as your nicotiana, petunias, and snapdragons. But if you're planting dahlia roots rather than plants, or in subsequent years if you've saved your own roots, here's what to do: Place each piece of root in the hole horizontally, cover with 1 inch of soil, and then tamp it down with your hands. Place a 2-foot wood or metal stake next to the crown end of the tuber. Gradually fill in the rest of the hole with soil as the dahlia sprouts and begins to grow. (See the illustration on page 245.)

Finally, plant the seeds for the California poppies, China asters, cornflowers, cosmos, four-o'clocks, marigolds, nasturtiums, pot marigolds, sunflowers, and zinnias. To sow the seed, rake the soil smooth in each circle. For smaller seeds, just scatter the seeds evenly over the plot and rake them in lightly or if you like, cover them with ½ inch of topsoil or vermiculite. For the larger sunflower, four-o'clock, and nasturtium seeds, press the seeds into the soil ¼ to ½ inch before you rake soil over them. After sowing, press down firmly with your hands so the seeds will be in contact with the soil.

Water this garden lightly on a daily or every-other-day basis for a week or two until the seeds germinate and begin to grow. Pull out any weeds to give the flowers all the room you can.

SEASON THREE (JUNE, JULY, AND AUGUST)

Minimize Chores and Enjoy Your Garden

Now that your garden is up and growing, there are three important tasks for you to take care of. First, thin your seedlings so the new plants stand 4 to 6 inches apart. When you thin, carefully pull the plants out by hand or snip them off at ground level with a sharp knife or garden scissors. Your new plants need room to grow, and thinning them is the best way to give it to them.

Next, snake your soaker hose through the garden in some form of an S-curve, covering as much of the garden as possible. Be sure to leave the connecting end of the hose visible so you can attach your regular garden hose to it.

Then, cover the garden, including the soaker hose, with a 2- to 4-inch-thick layer of natural organic mulch. The mulch will help control weeds and hold moisture in the soil. As it decomposes, it will add organic matter to the soil.

Most of these plants are very drought-tolerant and can withstand the abuse of a long, hot, dry summer once they are established. Water regularly until your plants are growing strongly, though. To water, simply connect your garden hose to the soaker hose and run the water for one to two hours, depending on how long it takes to soak the ground to a depth of 6 inches. Don't water your garden again for at least one week. It is important that you water deeply and infrequently to give your plants the chance to develop deep roots and to dry out between watering.

SEASON FOUR (SEPTEMBER AND OCTOBER)

Prepare the Garden for Winter

This is a very easy garden to prepare for winter. Just leave all the plants in the ground until frost kills them off. As the plants die, pull them up, shred them or break them up as much as possible, and add them to your compost bin. You can dig up and keep the glads and dahlias over winter and plant them again next year. (See "Prepare the Garden for Winter" on page 248 for how to store dahlias.)

Once all your annuals are dead, clear away any plant stems or roots. Remove the soaker hose, drain it, and store it for the winter. Till the soil with a rotary tiller or spade, turning all the partially decayed mulch into the soil. This fall tilling will help break down the organic matter and make the soil that much more friable, crumbly, and fertile for next year.

One of the things you might find in your garden next year are "volunteers," plants that have sprouted from seeds produced by your flowers. This is common with cosmos and marigolds and may even happen with zinnias and pot marigolds. Watch for sprouts of familiar leaves early next spring and then decide if you want to keep them.

Beautiful Easy Roses

A Garden of Gorgeous, Trouble-Free Roses

SURE, ROSES ARE BEAUTIFUL, but can they be easy to grow, too? The answer is a resounding yes! Growing roses does not have to be frustrating and labor-intensive. In fact, roses are actually easy to grow as long as you give them full sun and rich, well-drained soil. The secret to growing a beautiful easy rose garden is choosing the hardiest, most disease-resistant roses you can find.

This garden features some of the best rugged, trouble-free roses available. You'll find old-fashioned, fragrant climbers and beautiful, easy-care shrub roses that flower from early summer to fall.

15′ × 20′

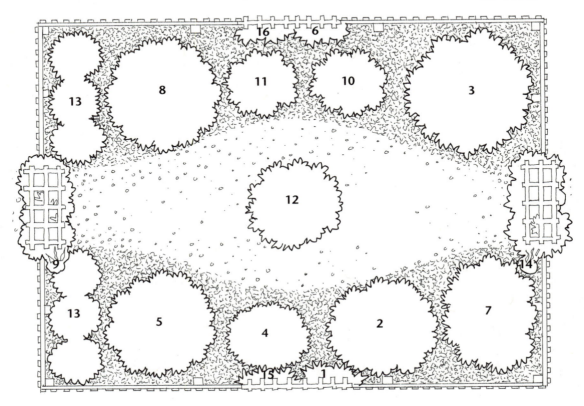

1. 'American Pillar' rose
2. 'Ballerina' rose
3. 'Blanc Double de Coubert' rose
4. 'The Fairy' rose
5. 'F. J. Grootendorst' rose
6. 'Golden Showers' rose
7. 'Graham Thomas' rose
8. 'Hansa' rose
9. 'New Dawn' rose
10. 'Othello' rose
11. 'Perdita' rose
12. 'Pink Meidiland' rose
13. 'Simplicity' roses
14. 'William Baffin' rose
15. Jackman clematis
16. 'Niobe' or other clematis

If you love roses, you'll be in heaven when you plant this beautiful easy rose garden.

RUGOSA ROSES TO BUY

Buy one of each of the following roses:

- 'Blanc Double de Coubert'
- 'F. J. Grootendorst'
- 'Hansa'

SHRUB ROSES TO BUY

Buy one of each of the following roses, unless otherwise noted:

- 'Ballerina'
- 'The Fairy'
- 'Pink Meidiland'
- 'Simplicity'. Buy six plants.

CLIMBING ROSES AND CLEMATIS TO BUY

Buy one of each of the following roses and clematis:

- 'American Pillar'
- 'Golden Showers'
- 'New Dawn'
- 'William Baffin'

- Jackman clematis
- 'Niobe', 'Hagley Hybrid', 'Ville de Lyon', or other clematis of your choice

ENGLISH ROSES TO BUY

Buy one of each of the following roses:

- 'Graham Thomas'
- 'Othello'
- 'Perdita'

THE PLANT GUIDE

PLANTS FOR A BEAUTIFUL EASY ROSE GARDEN

A LOT OF PEOPLE give up growing roses because they lavish hours and hours of care on them but still end up with scraggly looking plants. The problem is that they are trying to grow the wrong type of rose. Hybrid tea roses are the biggest culprits. Although they have beautiful flowers, many of them are susceptible to diseases and insects, and they also have a tough time surviving cold winters without a lot of protection. If you are willing to pamper them, hybrid tea roses can be very satisfying to grow.

You'll find that the roses in this garden are not only disease-resistant, but they also produce loads of flowers. They either bloom continually from early summer to fall or have a big flush of blooms in early summer and then bloom intermittently into fall. They are all quite hardy, too, and

need only a minimal amount of winter protection. Finally, they demand only the most minimal pruning—what a relief to those among us who are pruner-shy!

Climbing Roses

Buy one of each of the following climbing roses:

'American Pillar'. A classic rose introduced at the turn of the century, this rambler is still popular today. In early summer, it produces large clusters of pink flowers, each with a white eye. Canes generally reach 10 feet, but plants can climb to 15 or 20 feet if they're happy in the site you select. It is very disease-resistant and produces rose hips in the fall. Zones 5 to 9.

'Golden Showers'. The daffodil-yellow flowers of this rose fade to cream as they age. Although usually grown as a climber, 'Golden Showers' also can be grown as a shrub since its 6- to 7-foot canes are quite sturdy.

Plants have dark green leaves and produce a large flush of blooms in early summer, then bloom off and on through the fall. Zones 5 to 9.

'New Dawn'. Fragrant, cameo pink flowers decorate this disease-resistant climbing rose all summer long. It's one of the smaller climbing roses, producing 12- to 15-foot canes, which makes it a good choice for a smaller garden. Zones 5 to 9.

'William Baffin'. This versatile rose can be used either as a shrub or a climber. (Canes can reach over 10 feet.) It is extremely disease-resistant and bears semidouble pink flowers in early summer and then off and on through the fall. Zones 3 to 9.

English Roses

British rose hybridizer David Austin has developed a whole line of beautiful, tough roses that have fragrant, old-fashioned flowers and are disease-resistant. I've selected three of them for this garden; buy one of each.

'Graham Thomas'. This is one of my favorite English roses. It bears fragrant, golden yellow flowers in late spring, followed by sporadic blooming through the season. It is disease-resistant and grows 5 to 8 feet tall. Zones 5 to 9.

'Othello'. This David Austin hybrid bears fragrant, dark crimson blooms in early summer, then off and on through the fall. Plants can reach 6 to 8 feet and can be grown as shrubs or trained as climbers. Zones 5 to 9.

'Perdita'. Old-fashioned–looking apricot blooms appear on this repeat bloomer all summer long. Plants reach about 4 feet in height. Zones 5 to 9.

Rugosa Roses

Rugosa roses are among the toughest, most disease-resistant roses you can buy. They have attractive corrugated leaves, and they produce ornamental red rose hips in the fall. Buy one of each of the following rugosas:

'Blanc Double de Coubert'. This is a rugged bush, 4 to 5 feet tall and 4 feet wide, that produces lovely white semidouble flowers all summer long. The intensely fragrant flowers are followed by bright red hips that are showy into winter. It's also very hardy and disease-resistant. What more could you want? Zones 2 to 9.

'F. J. Grootendorst'. This rugosa bears large clusters of small (1- to 1½-inch) flowers that resemble carnations. The blooms are crimson and set off against very dark green foliage. It blooms profusely in spring, followed by repeat blooming throughout the season. Plants are relatively small for a rugosa, ranging from 3 to 5 feet. Zones 4 to 8.

Shrub Roses

Buy one of each of the following shrub roses, unless otherwise noted:

'Ballerina'. This 3- to 4-foot shrub is a hybrid musk rose that covers itself with huge clusters of delicate pink blossoms in early summer. Individual flowers are single with a white eye. They are slightly fragrant. Zones 5 to 9.

'The Fairy'. This is a classic rose that no garden should be without. It is a compact shrub that grows 2 to 3 feet tall and as wide. Plants are covered with large clusters of small pink flowers from summer to fall. It's a polyantha rose that's as at home in the perennial border or herb garden as it is in the rose garden. It's disease-resistant, too. Zones 4 to 9.

'Pink Meidiland'. The Meidiland series shrub roses are a relatively new development in the rose world. They're pest-resistant, adaptable shrubs that are great for a low-maintenance landscape. 'Pink Meidiland' is one of the best of the bunch. It is an everblooming shrub rose with clusters of single pink blossoms that look like wild roses. Plants are disease-resistant, although they probably aren't a good choice for the humid Deep South. The 4- to 5-foot plants bear orange-red rose hips in fall. Zones 4 to 8.

Many of the roses in this garden, including rugosa rose 'Blanc Double de Coubert', have gorgeous red rose hips in the late summer and fall. They are nearly as ornamental as the flowers and are even more attractive to birds and wildlife.

'Hansa'. This is a free-flowering rugosa with clove-scented double blooms that are dark mauve in color. Its biggest bloom time is late spring, but you'll get plenty of repeat bloom, too. 'Hansa' is a dense 5-foot shrub. Zones 3 to 8.

'**Simplicity**'. This is a shrublike floribunda rose that forms a low (2½- to 3½-foot), disease-resistant blooming hedge. The flowers are pink and bloom extravagantly in early summer and on and off until frost. Jackson and Perkins has sold 14 million of these very user-friendly roses so far! Buy six plants. Zones 5 to 9.

Clematis for Extra Bloom

I suggest that you buy two different clematis plants for this garden. The clematis vines happily entwine themselves on the sturdy rose canes, covering them with flowers in warm weather.

Jackman clematis (*Clematis × jackmanii*). This is probably the best known of the bunch. This vigorous vine produces large purple flowers in summer. Buy one plant to grow on the 'American Pillar' climbing rose. It is hardy in Zones 3 to 9.

The other clematis, which you'll pair with the 'Golden Showers' rose, is your choice. I would suggest ruby-red 'Niobe', floriferous pink 'Hagley Hybrid', or vivid red 'Ville de Lyon'. All are vigorous, heavy-blooming plants that will fill your garden with color at the time when your climbing roses are blooming only sporadically. All are hardy in Zones 3 to 9.

'Golden Showers' rose

'Ville de Lyon' clematis

Expert gardeners use a trick to make sure their climbing roses provide plenty of color through the summer: They grow them with clematis and let the rose canes serve double duty as a trellis.

THE SEASONAL GUIDE

SEASON ONE (JANUARY AND FEBRUARY)

Select a Site

January and February are good months to scout for an appropriate site for this garden. Roses need full sun, meaning no less than six hours of direct sun per day. However, don't be fooled by sites that look sunny when the leaves are off the trees at this time of year—your roses won't be. You can't give your roses too much sun, but with too little, they won't bloom and will be more prone to diseases. Roses also do best in a site that's open on all sides, which improves air circulation. That's why most rose gardens are located out in an open part of a yard or park, and yours should be, too.

Buy the Roses, Clematis, and Supplies

This 15 × 20-foot garden features a variety of low-maintenance roses and some clematis plants for extra bloom. Although you may be able to buy some of the plants from your local garden center, you'll get more for your money and a better selection if you order roses from one of the catalogs listed in "Where to Buy" on the opposite page.

In addition to the plants, you will need the following supplies to plant this garden:

• Four 40-pound bags of compost or composted manure. Or substitute homemade compost—one full bin or three wheelbarrows full.

• One 5-pound bag of natural organic fertilizer

• One 50-foot soaker hose, ¾ inch in diameter

• Six large bags of shredded organic mulch, such as pine bark, cedar bark, or pine needles. Or substitute an equivalent amount of your own compost, or a mix of compost and shredded leaves.

• 60 feet of 3-foot white picket fence

- Two 4 × 5-foot wooden trellises
- Two rose arbors
- One garden bench to fit under one of the arbors

You don't have to install a picket fence around this garden. All of the plants will grow wonderfully without it. I think it adds to the garden's appeal, though, so if you can afford it, by all means buy or build one.

You do need to buy or build the arbors and trellises, however. Otherwise the climbing roses will not have anything to climb on. If you like, you can improvise for the first year or two with temporary support. Then you can install permanent arbors and trellises when you have the time and money to do so.

SEASON TWO (MARCH, APRIL, AND MAY)

Prepare the Site

Before you start preparing your garden site, make sure the soil is no longer frozen and that it is dry enough to dig without forming muddy clumps. See "Getting Your Garden Ready to Plant" on page 42 for complete information on preparing the soil. (If you like, you can prepare the site for this garden in the fall and plant the following spring.)

WHERE TO BUY

You can order the roses for this garden from any of the following companies:

- Jackson & Perkins Co., 1 Rose Lane, Medford, OR 97501
- Roses of Yesterday & Today, 802 Brown's Valley Road, Watsonville, CA 95076
- Wayside Gardens, 1 Garden Lane, Hodges, SC 29695-0001
- White Flower Farm, P.O. Box 50, Litchfield, CT 06759-0050

Clear and mark off an area that is 15 feet wide and 20 feet long. As you can see from the design on page 120, most of the roses are planted on either side of a pathway that runs down the center of this garden. This pathway can be grass to mow, brick paving stones, or dark-colored crushed gravel.

Next, clear away any rocks and debris, and use a sharp garden spade to remove any grass that is growing there. Use the grass to patch spots in your lawn, or place it upside down on your compost pile. Then mark the pathway, including the circle in the center with stakes and string or a sprinkling of lime or flour. Spread the compost or composted manure and the fertilizer evenly over the rose planting beds, and dig the entire garden to a depth of 8 to 10 inches either by hand or with a rotary tiller.

Roses have big root systems, so the deeper you can dig the soil around them the better.

Once you've prepared the soil, install the white picket fence, the trellises, and the arbors next. It is best to dig up the soil before you install them, so you have room to maneuver when you are digging. (See the illus-

tration on this page for a suggestion on setting the posts in concrete and gravel.) Once you have installed them, rake the entire area smooth, and you are ready to plant.

Plant the Garden

As soon as there is no longer any danger of frost in your area, you can plant your rose garden. If you ordered your roses by mail, they should be shipped to you at the proper planting time for your area. When your roses arrive, generally you'll find dormant, bareroot plants. Since bareroot plants aren't potted, your roses will be wrapped in packing material like excelsior or paper and probably plastic. You have to be prepared to get those roses planted in the ground as quickly as you can. If you can't get them planted in a day or two, you must open up the package and add extra water to the packing material. Don't let them dry out or they might die. If you buy your roses in pots at your local nursery or garden center, all you have to do is keep the plants watered until the day you plant them.

The night before you are ready to plant, soak bareroot roses in a bucket of water to hydrate them before planting. (You'll need several buckets for this—washed-out, 5-gallon drywall-compound buckets work well

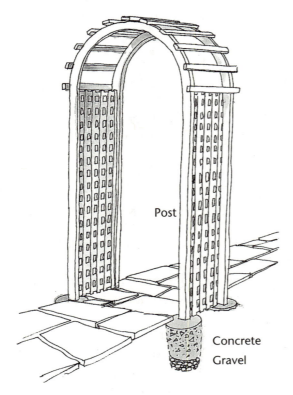

Post

Concrete

Gravel

Your climbing roses will thrive for years, so it pays to give them a trellis or arbor that will also last for many years. Use rot-resistant wood, such as cedar, and set the posts in concrete and gravel, as shown here.

for this because they're deep enough to immerse the roses to their crowns.) When planting day comes, bring all of your rose and clematis plants out to the garden. It's best to keep the roses soaking in water until just before you plant. If you are following my garden design on page 120 and want to mark individual planting sites, write the name of each rose on a different stake. Then put them in the planting sites.

Before you plant, read any planting instructions that accompanied your roses. Generally, all roses are planted in the same manner. Dig a hole that is larger and wider than the root system of the rose plant. Be sure to give the roots plenty of room to fit comfortably into the hole. For bareroot roses, build a cone of soil in the bottom of the hole and spread the roots over that.

Bareroot plants need to be planted so the bud union, if there is one, is slightly aboveground in warmer states and slightly below ground in colder ones. (Many of the roses in this garden are grown on their own roots and won't have a bud union, which looks like a little knob on the stem of the rose.) Potted roses should be planted so they will be growing at the same depth as they were in their pots.

Then start filling the hole with soil. You have already mixed organic matter and fertilizer into the soil, so

you don't need to make up any special mix. Firm the soil around the roots as you fill the hole. When the hole is half full of soil, water thoroughly. Then continue filling the hole, gathering soil around the roots and pressing down firmly with your hands.

Water the soil around the plant thoroughly until the ground is completely soaked. Don't cut corners and water all the plants at the end of your planting session—water each one as you plant, as I've described above. At this point, the more water the better, so take your time and rewater the newly planted roses several times to make sure they are really soaked.

Plant each clematis plant about 2 feet to the side of the climbing rose and at the base of the trellis. Dig a hole large enough to fit the clematis roots comfortably. Place the plant in the hole so that the crown, the area where the root zone meets the stems, is at ground level. Gather soil around the plant, press down firmly with your hands, and water the plant thoroughly until the ground is soaked.

Once you've got your plants and structures in place, it's time to add the most important feature—as far as your enjoyment is concerned, anyway! Position your garden bench under one of the arbors so you can sit surrounded by beautiful fragrant roses.

FEEDING AND PRUNING YOUR ROSES

Early spring, just as the new red buds begin to appear on the rosebushes, is the best time to prune your rosebushes. (This could be early March in the mid-South up to mid-April in northern areas.) The roses in this garden won't need much pruning, but you may need to remove a branch here and there. Here's what you need to know.

Climbing roses. Cut out dead or damaged wood and trim back the length of the canes until your climbers look the way you want them to. Otherwise, there is no real need to prune your climbing roses for several years.

Rugosa roses. The same goes for the rugosas. Prune out dead or damaged wood, and clip back branches here and there to direct their growth.

Shrub roses. The 'Simplicity' roses and the other shrub roses, including the Meidilands and English roses, also need very little pruning. But I do think you should prune off about one-third of their height each year to keep them looking their best and to improve the amount and quality of flowers they produce. (You can do this on the rugosas, too, if you like.)

After you have finished pruning, you can feed your plants. Sprinkle 2 tablespoons of Epsom salts, a good source of magnesium, at the base of each rose plant. (Epsom salts are many rose growers' "secret" ingredient for great-looking roses.) Sprinkle 1/4 cup of a balanced natural organic fertilizer over the salts, and work them both into the soil with your fingers. Spread an additional 2 to 4 inches of dehydrated or composted manure or regular compost around the base of each rosebush. Now your roses are ready to grow for another year.

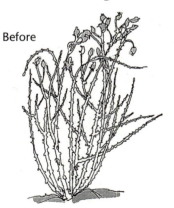

Before

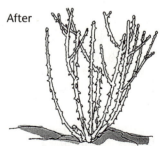

After

Whenever you prune, use clean, sharp bypass pruners and make cuts at a 45-degree angle just above a healthy outward-facing bud. Prune out any dead, broken, or damaged stems below the area where the damage occurred and above a healthy bud.

The last step is to snake your soaker hose through the garden, making sure it will water each and every plant. Then spread a 2- to 4-inch layer of natural organic mulch over the soaker hose and the garden bed to stifle weeds and hold in moisture. Be sure to keep the connecting end of the soaker hose visible so you can find it.

Keep all of your newly planted roses and clematis watered—every few days is best if you don't have ample rain, at least until the plants have recovered from the shock of transplanting and are growing strongly. Ample watering makes a big difference in getting your roses established and growing well.

SEASON THREE (JUNE, JULY, AND AUGUST)

Minimize Chores and Enjoy Your Garden

Summer maintenance of roses is incredibly easy. Once your plants are well established and growing strongly, water the garden no more than once a week. To water, simply connect the soaker hose to a conventional garden hose and turn on the water for one hour. This will slowly soak the ground, providing ample moisture for the plants. If you have at least ½ inch of rain during a week, you don't need to water your roses.

You will need to train your climbing roses onto the trellises and arbors. Simply select two or three of the sturdiest canes, and gently attach them to the slats or pillars with string or green twine, spreading them out so they will cover as much of the wood structure as possible.

Your climbing roses may or may not grow very much during the first or even second year. It may take them a few years to cover the trellises or arbors in this garden. Be patient, keep them watered, and they will soon take off and bloom like crazy for many years.

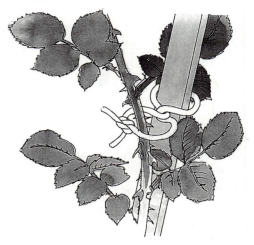

Use soft string and a figure-eight knot to tie up rose canes. Make sure the loop isn't too tight around the cane.

All of the roses in this garden are known to be resistant to diseases — including mildew and black spot — so you will not have to spend any time worrying about disease control.

Aphids might attack your roses. When they do, spray them off with a hard, direct spray of water from the hose. If that doesn't work, use insecticidal soap. Eventually lady beetles will move in and control the problem for you if you avoid using anything stronger than water sprays.

If you live in certain areas of the country, Japanese beetles may attack your roses. Hire the neighborhood kids to pick them off by hand and squish them or drop them in a bucket of soapy water — or do the chore yourself. Pyrethrum is also effective on Japanese beetles, although it's best to avoid it since it also kills beneficial insects.

I've found that most roses, even the everblooming kind, tend to have a huge bloom in spring and early summer and then bloom sporadically all summer long. Fall usually brings on another pretty big bloom cycle. Since deadheading to remove spent flowers prevents ornamental rose hips from forming, I just shake the bushes lightly after a big bloom cycle to knock off the dead or dying rose petals. This seems to make room for new blooms.

When you cut roses for bouquets, do a little pruning, too — cut just above a leaf that points out rather than into the center of the bush. This encourages your roses to stay open in the center, improving air circulation.

SEASON FOUR (SEPTEMBER AND OCTOBER)

Prepare the Garden for Winter

Many of these roses will continue blooming on into the fall. I have had some of my roses take a few light frosts and keep right on blooming.

Tie the canes of your climbing roses to the trellises or arbors with string or twine. This prevents them from whipping around during storms.

Remove the soaker hose, drain it, and store it for the winter.

Don't do anything to winterize your roses until they have completely stopped blooming and the ground is beginning to freeze or get as cold as it gets in your area. It is important that your roses are fully dormant before you add winter protection. Then place an additional 2 to 4 inches of compost at the base of each rosebush. If your area receives a natural blanket of snow each winter, that is perfect protection also.

A Shady Woodland Wildflower Garden

Beautiful Ways to Light Up a Shady Site

OUR NATIVE WOODLAND WILDFLOWERS have a charm and beauty that are all their own. This wildflower garden will thrive in a shady backyard.

Early-spring wildflowers, including bluebells, columbines, bleeding hearts, and Jack-in-the-pulpits, provide the first wave of color. They're followed by native evergreen shrubs that form a backdrop for this woodland setting and bloom in late spring. Wildflowers such as Solomon's plumes and wild cranebills, along with ferns and other foliage plants, keep the garden appealing through the fall.

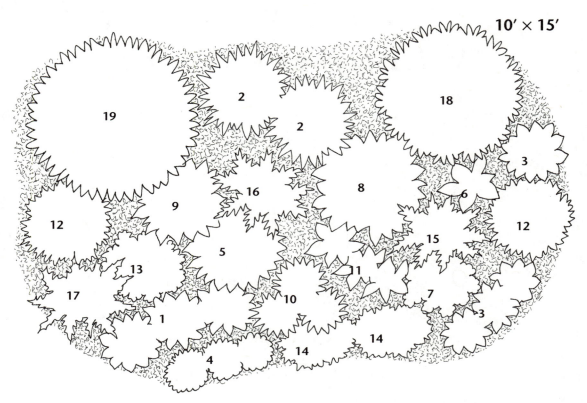

10′ × 15′

1. Allegheny foam-flowers
2. Black snakeroots
3. Canada wild gingers
4. Dutchman's breeches
5. Great blue lobelia
6. Jack-in-the-pulpit
7. 'Palace Purple' heuchera
8. Pink turtlehead
9. Solomon's plume
10. Virginia bluebells
11. White trilliums
12. Wild bleeding heart
13. Wild columbine
14. Wild cranesbills
15. Cinnamon fern
16. Lady fern
17. Maidenhair fern
18. Carolina rhododendron
19. Mountain laurel

You don't need a woodland to enjoy this beautiful wildflower garden—just a shade tree or two.

FERNS TO BUY
Buy one of each of the following ferns:
- Cinnamon fern
- Lady fern
- Maidenhair fern

SHRUBS TO BUY
Buy one of each of the following shrubs:
- Carolina rhododendron
- Mountain laurel

PLANTS TO BUY
Buy one of each of the following wild-flowers, unless otherwise noted:
- Allegheny foamflowers. Buy three.
- Black snakeroots. Buy two.
- Canada wild gingers. Buy four.
- Dutchman's breeches. Buy three.
- Great blue lobelia
- Jack-in-the-pulpit
- 'Palace Purple' heuchera
- Pink turtlehead
- Solomon's plume
- Virginia bluebells. Buy three.
- White trilliums. Buy three.
- Wild bleeding heart. Buy two.
- Wild columbine
- Wild cranesbills. Buy two.

THE PLANT GUIDE

PLANTS FOR A WOODLAND GARDEN

THIS GARDEN features handsome foliage and beautiful flowers for weeks on end. Evergreen shrubs ensure that you'll have a cheerful spot of green on even the bleakest winter day. And from early spring on, flowers and foliage will provide endless appeal.

Plants

Buy one of each of the following wildflowers, unless otherwise noted:

Allegheny foamflower (*Tiarella cordifolia*). Allegheny foamflower makes a very attractive woodland groundcover that spreads quickly to form large mats. Plants range from 6 to 10 inches and form mounds of nearly triangular, sharp-toothed leaves. Spikes of fluffy white flowers appear in early spring. Buy three plants. Zones 3 to 8.

Black snakeroot (*Cimicifuga racemosa*). Also called bugbane and black cohosh, this striking woodland wildflower ranges from 4 to 7 feet tall. It sends up spikes of fluffy white flowers in August and September. Buy two plants. Zones 3 to 8.

Canada wild ginger (*Asarum canadense*). Satiny, heart-shaped leaves, a low-growing habit, and the ability to spread quickly make this a great woodland groundcover. Look under the 6- to 12-inch foliage in spring for the tiny purple flower borne next to the soil. Buy four plants. Zones 3 to 8.

Dutchman's breeches (*Dicentra cucullaria*). Like its relative, wild bleeding heart, this dainty little woodland plant has ferny foliage. The white flowers are borne in spring and resemble billowy pantaloons hanging upside down on the line to dry. Plants are 10 to 12 inches tall and, like many spring wild-flowers, die back after flowering. Buy three plants. Zones 3 to 8.

Great blue lobelia (*Lobelia siphilitica*). A cousin to red cardinal flower, great blue lobelia bears sky-blue flowers in mid- to late summer. Plants reach 3 feet when mature and will spread. Zones 4 to 8.

Jack-in-the-pulpit (*Arisaema triphyllum*). Unique is the best way to describe this 2-foot woodland native.

Three-lobed leaves partly conceal the exotic-looking green-and-white striped flower that resembles a preacher in a pulpit. Jack-in-the-pulpit dies down during the summer and then produces a golf-ball–size spike of densely packed, showy red berries. Zones 3 to 9.

'Palace Purple' heuchera (*Heuchera micrantha* var. *diversifolia* 'Palace Purple'). While not technically a wildflower, 'Palace Purple'

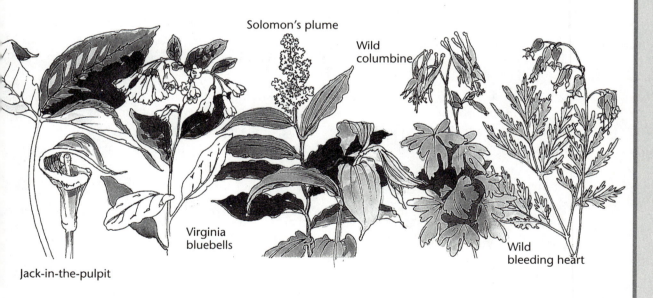

Solomon's plume

Wild columbine

Virginia bluebells

Wild bleeding heart

Jack-in-the-pulpit

Spring wildflower gardens will be filled with flowers before your trees even leaf out. Early-blooming native wildflowers like these thrive in the spring sunshine under deciduous trees as well as in the summer shade they cast.

heuchera is an improved selection of a West Coast native. But since its foliage is so stunning—the leaves are maplelike in shape and purple-brown or bronze-red in color, depending on how you look at them—I decided to include it anyway. The leaves add color to the front of the garden from spring through fall, and the 1-foot plants are topped by delicate white flowers in midsummer. Zones 4 to 8.

Pink turtlehead (*Chelone lyonii*). Dark green foliage sets off the pink flowers of this vigorous wildling quite nicely. Flowers, each shaped like a turtle's head with its mouth agape, appear in late summer and early fall on 1- to 3-foot plants. Zones 3 to 8.

Solomon's plume (*Smilacina racemosa*). Also called false Solomon's seal because of its resemblence to another native woodlander, Solomon's plume bears a cloud of creamy white blooms in a feathery plume atop 2- to 3-foot plants. Dark green leaves set the flowers off nicely. The late-spring flowers are followed by red berries, and the plants spread by roots as well as reseeding. Zones 3 to 8.

Virginia bluebells (*Mertensia virginica*). This woodland wildflower bears clusters of pink buds that open into nodding, light blue flowers. After the 1- to 2-foot plants bloom in early spring, they disappear for the summer. Buy three plants. Zones 3 to 9.

White trillium (*Trillium grandiflorum*). Showy white flowers in spring and large bright green leaves make white trillium a delightful addition to any wildflower garden. The flowers of these 1½- to 2-foot plants turn a soft pink as they age. Before you buy, though, be sure to check that the plants you are being offered are nursery-propagated, not collected in the wild. See "Where to Buy" on page 142 for a list of reputable dealers. Buy three plants. Zones 3 to 9.

Wild bleeding heart (*Dicentra eximia*). Despite its delicate looks, wild bleeding heart is a tough, easy-to-grow wildflower. Two-foot mounds of ferny foliage are topped by clusters of dangling pink or white heart-shaped blooms. The main show is in the spring, but the plants rebloom throughout the summer if the weather isn't too hot. Buy two plants. Zones 3 to 9.

Wild columbine (*Aquilegia canadensis*). A dainty wild relative of hybrid garden columbines, this spring-blooming woodland native bears nodding red-and-yellow flowers on 1- to 3-foot plants. It will self-sow and spread. Zones 3 to 8.

Wild cranesbill (*Geranium maculatum*). This easy-to-grow wildflower bears dainty pink flowers on 1- to 2-foot plants. It begins blooming in late spring and can continue on and off through the summer in cooler areas. Buy two plants— they'll spread. Zones 4 to 8.

Ferns

What would a woodland garden be without ferns to add their delicate beauty? From the fascinating fiddleheads that unfurl in spring through the often statuesque russet foliage that adds garden interest through the fall and winter, ferns are really four-season plants. The more you look at ferns, the more you'll appreciate them. Buy one of each of the following ferns:

Cinnamon fern (*Osmunda cinnamomea*). This vigorous fern forms clumps of fronds 3 feet tall or taller. (The wetter the soil, the taller the fronds—they can reach 5 or 6 feet in height.) The common name refers to the cinnamon-colored fertile fronds that appear in late summer. The plant will spread. Zones 4 to 9.

Lady fern (*Athyrium filix-femina*). This delicate-looking fern has lacy, 2-foot fronds that are pale green. The plants usually form circular clumps. Zones 4 to 9.

Maidenhair fern (*Adiantum pedatum*). Delicate blue-green fronds adorn this 2-foot woodland beauty. Each frond is circular or horseshoe-shaped. The plant will spread by creeping roots if it's happy where it is planted. Zones 3 to 8.

Shrubs

Buy one of each of the following shrubs:

Carolina rhododendron (*Rhododendron carolinianum*). Unlike the gaudier hybrid rhododendrons that you see everywhere in the spring, this 6-foot native evergreen shrub has thinner leaves and more natural-looking blossoms that vary in color from white to pale rose or deep pink. It blooms in May or June. Zones 5 to 7.

Mountain laurel (*Kalmia latifolia*). Mountain laurel is truly one of our most beautiful native shrubs. It has leathery, evergreen leaves and a treelike habit at maturity (it can reach 15 feet tall). It bears clusters of pink, white, or red cup-shaped flowers that appear in late spring after most of the popular spring bloomers are finished for the year. Zones 5 to 9.

THE SEASONAL GUIDE

SEASON ONE (JANUARY AND FEBRUARY)

WILDFLOWERS can be intimidating. They seem so delicate and temperamental. But this is actually a very easy garden to prepare, plant, and take care of. First of all, there are no seeds to buy, start indoors, or plant outside. You will plant either a container-grown perennial or shrub.

Two elements of this garden, finding the right site and finding all the plants you want, might be a little trickier. I hope I can help you overcome these two hurdles to make your backyard woodland garden a great success.

Select a Site

You may have to do some prowling around in your backyard to select the right site for this garden. Start by looking for an area that re-sembles the natural woodlands that appear in your area. (You might find it helpful to go for a walk in the park or on a nature trail to refresh your memory of what woodlands look like in your part of the country.)

For this woodland garden, you need a site that is in partial to full shade. That means it will receive no sun or only the sunlight filtered down through the leaves and branches of tall trees. (In early spring, before deciduous trees leaf out, the right site will seem quite sunny, though.) The plants in this garden also need soil that is rich in organic matter and stays moist all summer long.

Ideally, you want a spot under or near medium-size trees—either one tree or, better yet, clumps of several different trees. Birches, crabapples, dogwoods, or redbuds are ideal. Sites under taller trees, including ashes and oaks, form great settings, too. Unfortunately, shallow-rooted trees like maples crowd the soil with their roots and tend to suck out all the available moisture, making it harder to garden under them. But I have a woodland garden under a maple tree and everything is doing quite nicely—thanks to a heavy mulch and my soaker hose—so don't give up hope.

If you don't have any trees, look for a site on the north side of your garage or house. You'll find that the buildings can create some shade for most of the day.

Because everyone's yard is different, don't limit yourself to a site that will accommodate the garden I've drawn for this book. Instead, use my design as a jumping-off point. The garden you create may twist and turn like a snake, it may be long and narrow, or it may curve like a crescent roll. Let your site help you decide on the best shape.

Buy Plants and Supplies

The best places to buy the plants for this garden are mail-order nurseries that specialize in growing their own wildflowers. Write away for catalogs now so you can order plants in plenty of time for spring.

Whatever you do, don't buy from nurseries that collect plants from the

---

GET INTO WILDFLOWERS

Once you've grown wildflowers, you'll undoubtedly be bitten by the wildflower bug. To learn more about the wildflowers in your region, you may want to join a local native plant society or investigate the classes offered at a local botanical garden. Both often hold native plant sales, too.

Also consider writing for membership information from the following organizations:

• The National Wildflower Research Center, 2600 FM 973 North, Austin, TX 78725

• The New England Wild Flower Society, Garden in the Woods, 180 Hemenway Road, Framingham, MA 01701-2699

---

wild. Don't go out and dig your own plants either. The best home for wildflowers is where they grow naturally in the wild. But you can get the plants you want without depleting wild areas. You'll find a list of nurseries that propagate their own wildflowers in "Where to Buy" on page 142.

You may also want to see what wildflowers are offered at local garden centers. Their offerings may surprise you. But look carefully at the plants and ask questions about where they came from. Nursery-grown plants will look like they've been growing in pots all their lives—because they have been. Plants that look stuffed into pots, have irregular shapes, or have lots of broken foliage probably were collected in the wild. Native shrubs aren't immune from collectors either. Balled-and-burlapped plants that have craggy, irregular branching habits have been probably collected from the wild, too.

In addition to the plants listed for this garden, you'll need the following supplies:

• Four 40-pound bags of compost or composted manure. Or substitute homemade compost—one full bin or three wheelbarrows full.

• Two 4-cubic-foot bags of additional organic matter, such as compost, chopped leaves, or rotted sawdust

• One 5-pound bag of natural organic fertilizer

• One 25-foot soaker hose, ¾ inch in diameter

• Four large bags of shredded organic mulch, such as pine bark, cedar bark, or pine needles. Or substitute an equivalent amount of your own compost or a mix of compost and shredded leaves.

SEASON TWO
(MARCH, APRIL, AND MAY)

Prepare the Site

Once you've found the right site, you need to prepare the soil. You can start this process in late February in southern states. In the North, you can begin removing weeds on a warm winter day when the soil has thawed a bit. But for the most part, you'll want to prepare the soil now. Another option is to make planting and installation a three-season process: Prepare the soil in the fall and mulch the site over winter. Then pull back the mulch and plant in the spring.

The key to this garden is soil that resembles the soil found in the

---

WHERE TO BUY

The following nurseries offer nursery-propagated wildflowers:

• Brookside Wildflowers, Route 3, Box 740, Boone, NC 28607

• Native Gardens, 5737 Fisher Lane, Greenback, TN 37742

• We-Du Nurseries, Route 5, Box 724, Marion, NC 28752

---

woods. It needs to be very rich in organic matter, including compost, shredded leaves, composted manure, and ground or shredded bark. These woodland plants prefer a slightly acid soil. (Most soils in the eastern half of the United States are slightly acid.) Have your soil pH tested by your local Cooperative Extension Service office (listed under city or county governments in your telephone book), or buy a home-test kit and do it yourself. Unless your soil is seriously alkaline, above 7.5 on the pH scale, I don't recommend adding any sulfur to lower it. Adding plenty of organic matter, such as compost and shredded leaves or pine bark, will lower the pH enough to make this soil perfect for wildflowers.

Because the garden site is under or near trees and shrubs, you won't be able to till the soil with a rotary tiller. A tiller would simply damage tree roots and bog down. Fortunately, wildflowers are accustomed to growing near the base of trees, and even the shrubs in this garden are relatively shallow-rooted because they're natural shade growers as well.

Once you have chosen and outlined your site, clear out any grass or debris and then start digging the area with a garden fork or spade. If you hit a root, just leave it and work around it. You are only trying to loosen the soil as best you can.

Break up the soil and smooth it out as much as you can without

Root-filled soil is inevitable when you're planting under trees and shrubs. When planting wildflowers or other shade lovers, use a trowel to gently look for deeper soil between roots to use as planting pockets.

damaging tree roots. Add the entire bag of natural organic fertilizer, the compost, and the other organic matter and incorporate them into the soil. You are basically trying to raise the soil level up 2 or 3 inches so that when you do plant, you won't be in conflict with the tree roots.

Plant the Garden

Your site will have a major effect on where you put each plant in your garden. Tree roots alone may require some adaptations. Be prepared to adjust the shape of your garden and the exact location of each plant, using the garden design on page 134 as a guideline.

The shrubs should serve as the visual backdrop of the garden, so select positions for them first. They will define the space and provide a natural setting for the other plants. When fully mature, they will be 5 to 6 feet tall and their branches and evergreen leaves will be visible all winter long. The black snakeroot plants are also large plants and need to be in the back of the garden. Everything else is small and can be tucked in here and there to fit your landscape design.

Here's a neat touch for your woodland wildflower garden: You can customize the design and make it more natural-looking by adding a few medium to large stones, a short piece of tree limb, or a log to your garden. Add them before you position the perennials and ferns.

All of the plants in this garden are hardy shrubs, ferns, and perennials, but there is no sense planting them until the ground is free of frost and the soil is warm enough to work. These plants won't be bothered by a late spring frost, though, so by all means plant before the last frost date, if you can. That way you can enjoy at least some of your wildflowers' blooms the first year.

When you're ready to plant, take all of the plants out to the garden site. Arrange them in the spots where you want to plant them, either using the design on page 134 or your own design. For my design, the mountain laurel goes at one end of the garden and the Carolina rhododendron at the other. The black snakeroot plants are placed between them, also at the back of the garden. Place the next row of plants—the bleeding heart, Solomon's plume, cinnamon fern, pink turtle-head, Jack-in-the-pulpit, and lady fern—3 feet in front of the shrubs and space them equally.

The next arc of plants—the maidenhair fern, wild columbine, great blue lobelia, Virginia bluebells, trilliums, 'Palace Purple' heuchera, and wild ginger plants—go 3 feet in front of the last row and are also evenly spaced. Finish up by placing the Allegheny foamflowers, Dutchman's breeches, and wild cranesbills across the front border of the garden.

Before you actually plant, step back and look at the garden from several angles to see if you like the arrangement. Then, starting at the back of the garden, put each plant in the site you've selected by digging a hole large enough to hold the root ball. (If you have bareroot plants, make sure there is enough room to spread the roots out in the hole.) Make each hole only deep enough so the crown of the plant—the point where the top of the plant meets the roots—is at ground level. To refill the hole, gather the soil around the plant and press down firmly with your hands. Water thoroughly.

After all the plants are in position, place the soaker hose in the garden by snaking it around to cover as much of the garden as possible. Be sure to leave the connecting end visible. Then cover the entire garden, including the hose, with a 2- to 4-inch layer of the organic mulch. Keep the mulch 1 inch away from all the perennials and ferns and 2 inches away from the trunks of the shrubs to discourage rot.

SEASON THREE (JUNE, JULY, AND AUGUST)

Minimize Chores and Enjoy Your Garden

Maintenance for this garden is almost nil. These plants will require watering on a frequent basis, though, especially until they're established.

No more than once a week, attach the soaker hose to your conventional garden hose and run the water for an hour. This along with average rainfall should be enough moisture to keep these plants happy. If the weather has been particularly dry and the plants seem to be suffering, run the soaker hose for two hours instead of one.

You really don't have to do anything else all summer long because the spring-blooming plants die back and disappear for the most part and the summer plants come on next. Don't panic—they'll be back next spring!

Just be aware that many of these plants will not bloom the first year. Instead, they spend the first season getting accustomed to their new site and putting down roots. They will return next year, ready to show off their blossoms. Don't worry if the shrubs bloom only sporadically for the first couple of years; they often take longer to become established. Just keep them mulched and watered, and they'll settle in and begin blooming in their own time.

Add additional mulch if the soil begins to show through. This garden will be rich with microorganisms and they will eat up the organic matter and mulch in no time at all.

SEASON FOUR (SEPTEMBER AND OCTOBER)

Prepare the Garden for Winter

You really don't have to do much to prepare this garden for winter, either. (I said this was an easy garden, didn't I?) After the cold weather has arrived and the perennials are brown, cut them back to the ground. Remove the soaker hose, drain it, and store it for the winter.

To replenish the mulch on the garden and help your wildflowers feel as if they're growing on the forest floor, collect leaves with a bagging mower, then sprinkle a light, 1- to 2-inch layer of shredded leaves over the garden. In fact, if you add a 1-inch layer of compost each spring and a 2-inch layer of shredded leaves each fall, you won't need to do anything else to this garden except enjoy it for years to come. Even the shrubs will not need to be pruned for several years, if at all.

A Beautiful Easy Butterfly Garden

Butterflies Make
This Garden Twice as Colorful

IT'S EASY TO ROLL OUT the welcome mat for butterflies. All you have to do is grow the kinds of flowers they need for food and shelter. Butterflies like the sun, too, so this is a full-sun garden.

This garden features many brightly colored flowers that butterflies adore. In the summer, there's orange butterfly weed, purple coneflowers, yellow and orange marigolds and nasturtiums, and red bee balm. In the fall, pinks and purples predominate as butterfly bush and asters come into bloom. And, of course, the butterflies add a layer of color that floats over all the flowers.

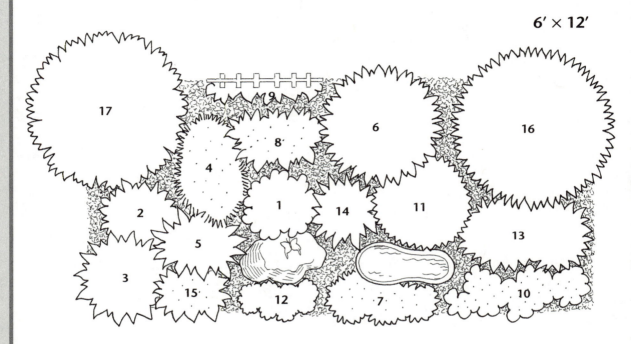

6′ × 12′

1. 'Autumn Joy' sedum
2. Bee balm
3. Butterfly weed
4. Cosmos
5. Gloriosa daisy
6. Joe-Pye weed

7. Marigolds
8. Mexican sunflowers
9. Morning glories
10. Nasturtiums
11. New England aster
12. Parsley

13. Phlox
14. Purple coneflower
15. Zinnias
16. Butterfly bush
17. Lilac

You'll love the "floating flowers" that will come to visit your beautiful easy butterfly garden.

SEEDS TO BUY

Buy one packet of each of the following annuals:

- Cosmos
- Marigolds
- Mexican sunflowers
- Morning glories
- Nasturtiums
- Zinnias

PLANTS TO BUY

Buy one of each of the following perennials or biennials:

- 'Autumn Joy' sedum
- Bee balm
- Butterfly weed
- Gloriosa daisy
- Joe-Pye weed
- New England aster
- Parsley
- Phlox
- Purple coneflower

SHRUBS TO BUY

Buy one of each of the following shrubs:

- Butterfly bush
- Lilac

THE PLANT GUIDE

PLANTS FOR A BEAUTIFUL EASY BUTTERFLY GARDEN

SINCE butterflies need to eat from late spring through early fall, this garden was planned to provide flowers for butterflies over a long season. (And what gardener would object to a garden that blooms for months on end?) The lilac blooms first, followed by summer-blooming annuals like cosmos, marigolds, Mexican sunflowers, and zinnias, which flower until frost—especially if you remember to remove their spent flowers. Perennials such as butterfly weeds, phlox, and purple coneflowers light up the garden in the summer, too. In the fall, butterfly bush, Joe-Pye weed, New England asters, and 'Autumn Joy' sedum take center stage in the garden. And since to have butterflies you have to have caterpillars, this garden design includes plants for them, too.

One of the great things about growing a butterfly-attracting garden is that butterflies don't like gardens that are very tidy. These are wild creatures that are accustomed to living in fields and meadows. They are happier in a garden that reminds them of their natural home. So relax, enjoy your garden, and tell your neighbors you're doing it for the butterflies!

Seeds

Buy one packet of each of the following annuals:

Cosmos (*Cosmos* spp.). Butterflies love the daisylike flowers of these easy-to-grow annuals. For this garden, I recommend garden cosmos (*C. bipinnatus*), which has white, pink, lavender-pink, and magenta flowers. Plants reach 3 to 4 feet and are nicely branched with feathery leaves. Don't buy one of the dwarf cultivars; instead, look for a tall cultivar, which is easy to find. There are some specially bred as cut flowers, so choose them if you enjoy indoor arrangements.

Marigolds (*Tagetes* spp.). Most gardeners have grown marigolds at one time or another. They're a terrific addition to any butterfly garden and one of the easiest annuals to grow. Butterflies will appreciate any type you choose, but for this garden I suggest double French marigolds, such as 'Queen Sophia', which has deep orange petals edged in yellow, or single dwarf French types, such as 'Naughty Marietta', which has yellow flowers splashed with maroon. Signet marigolds, such as 'Golden Gem' or 'Lemon Gem', are fine, too. All mature between 8 and 12 inches tall.

Mexican sunflowers (*Tithonia rotundifolia*). These bushy annuals attract butterflies like magnets. The gorgeous, daisylike flowers are bright orange to scarlet and are carried on tall, somewhat rangy, 4- to 5-foot plants. 'Sundance' and 'Torch' are good cultivars; 'Goldfinger' is an attractive compact one that ranges from 3 to 3½ feet tall at maturity.

Morning glories (*Ipomoea* spp.). Morning glories are climbing annuals that can reach as far as 15 feet. Look for a packet that offers a mix of blue, white, pink, and red. They'll clamber up the trellis in the back of this garden.

Nasturtiums (*Tropaeolum majus*). These colorful annuals are perfect edging plants for a butterfly garden. They tolerate drought and poor soil, yet cover themselves with colorful red, orange, and yellow blooms all summer. The leaves and flowers are peppery-tasting and great when added to salads. For this garden, buy either 'Alaska', which has green leaves variegated with white, or plants in the Jewel series. Both are between 8 and 12 inches tall.

Zinnias (*Zinnia elegans*). Zinnias are another butterfly favorite. And you can't beat them for summer-long color and flowers for cutting—as long as you give them plenty of sun. For this garden, look for any cultivars that are about 2 feet tall. You'll have your pick of reds, pinks, lavenders, yellows, and whites. If you can find the all-green cultivar 'Envy', by all means give it a try.

Plants

Buy one of each of the following biennials or perennials:

'Autumn Joy' sedum (*Sedum* 'Autumn Joy'). In the fall, the flowers of this classic perennial are covered with butterflies and bees. Plants form attractive 2-foot mounds that have all-season interest. They have fleshy green leaves followed by flat-topped

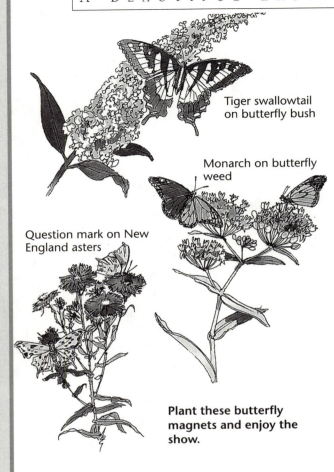

Tiger swallowtail on butterfly bush

Monarch on butterfly weed

Question mark on New England asters

Plant these butterfly magnets and enjoy the show.

flowers adorn the 2- to 4-foot plants for most of the summer. The minty, pungent-leaved plants are vigorous spreaders, and both the flowers and leaves make nice additions to teas and potpourri. For this garden, I suggest a pink- or white-flowered one, such as 'Croftway Pink' or 'Marshall's Delight' (both pink), or 'Snow White'. Plants will spread. Zones 4 to 8.

Butterfly weed (*Asclepias tuberosa*). A colorful relative of common milkweed, butterfly weed attracts monarchs and dozens of other butterflies like a magnet. It is a deep-rooted native wildflower found in fields throughout much of the eastern half of the country. It produces clusters of bright orange flowers all summer long atop 2- to 3-foot plants. Zones 3 to 9.

Gloriosa daisy (*Rudbeckia hirta* 'Gloriosa Daisy'). This is a cultivated variation on our native black-eyed Susan. The plants bear golden yellow flowers variously marked with oranges, rusts, and browns that appear from midsummer to frost. Flowers have brown centers and may be single or double. Plants grow to 2 feet tall. Gloriosa daisies are usually grown as annuals or biennials, although since they'll usually reseed in your garden, they behave like peren-

clusters of green flower buds that turn pink and then mature to bronze in the fall. The dried flowers will stand in the garden until you remove them in late winter, or you can use them in dried flower arrangements. Zones 3 to 9.

Bee balm (*Monarda didyma*). Bee balm attracts as many butterflies as it does bees. Red, pink, or white

nials. (They're easy from seed, but starting with a plant or two gives more color a bit faster.) If you like, you can substitute the perennial orange coneflower (*R. fulgida*), which is hardy in Zones 3 to 9.

Joe-Pye weed (*Eupatorium purpureum*). Swallowtails are especially fond of this native, fall-blooming perennial. Plants range from 3 to 6 feet tall, depending on how much moisture they get, and the huge clouds of light purple flowers appear in late summer and early fall. If you can't find *E. purpureum*, look for either *E. maculatum* or *E. fistulosum*. Zones 3 to 8.

New England aster (*Aster novae-angliae*). Butterflies and bees congregate on this native, fall-blooming wildflower. Plants can reach 4 feet or more and bear daisylike flowers in red, purple, pink, and lavender-blue. Buy whatever color appeals to you. 'Alma Potschke' has dark pink flowers, 'Hella Lacy' has royal purple, and 'Treasure' has lavender-blue. Plants will spread. Zones 3 to 8.

Parsley (*Petroselinum crispum*). Parsley foliage provides food for swallowtail butterfly babies (better known as caterpillars), so I always plant enough for both of us. Although it is fairly easy to grow from seed, I find it easier to buy a pot or six-pack of plants at the local garden center. The plants grow to about 12 inches tall. Parsley is biennial, but plants will overwinter and reseed as far north as Zone 6.

Phlox (*Phlox paniculata*). Garden phlox is another butterfly plant. Isn't it nice that butterflies like so many pretty flowers? Plants bear domed clusters of magenta, pink, or white flowers on 2- to 3-foot plants in the summer. Look for the mildew-resistant cultivars, including 'David', 'Franz Schubert', 'Eva Cullum', and 'Omega'. Zones 3 or 4 to 8.

Purple coneflower (*Echinacea purpurea*). This native American wildflower produces daisylike blooms all summer with the surprising combination of purplish pink petals and orange-brown centers. White-flowered cultivars are also available. Plants reach 2 to 4 feet. Zones 3 to 8.

Shrubs

Buy one of each of the following shrubs:

Butterfly bush (*Buddleia davidii*). Although butterfly bush dies back to the ground each winter, the plant is so large and bushy that it's generally treated as a shrub. Plants reach up to 4 feet tall and wide. The blooms, which appear from midsummer until frost, look like small lilacs; they even come in some of the same colors—lavender, red-violet, and purple. The blossoms attract butterflies like magnets. Zones 5 to 9.

Lilac (*Syringa vulgaris*). Lilac is a wonderful old-fashioned shrub or small tree that bears intensely fragrant flowers in early to mid-spring. Nearly everyone has seen a lilac with pale lavender blooms, but there are also cultivars with deep purple, pink, white, and even magenta flowers. Unfortunately, the leaves often get covered with unattractive powdery mildew during the summer. But butterflies love lilacs because they bear their flowers so early in the spring. Zones 3 to 7.

If you don't want to plant a lilac in this garden, consider **sweet mock orange** (*Philadelphus coronarius*), another butterfly favorite. Mock orange is also an old-fashioned shrub, and it bears clouds of very fragrant white flowers on plants that can reach 10 or 12 feet and spread as far. It blooms in May or June. Zones 4 to 8.

THE SEASONAL GUIDE

SEASON ONE (JANUARY AND FEBRUARY)

Select a Site

January and February are good months to scout for a site that will appeal to butterflies and the flowers they enjoy. You will need an area that is about 6 feet wide and 12 feet long. Your site needs to be in full sun for at least six hours a day. A sunny site on the east or south side of your house is ideal. Butterflies especially like sites that are sunny in the morning, since they must use the sun to warm their bodies before they can start flying in the morning. During the day, butterflies like to rest in open locations that are warm and sunny.

When you are out looking for a site, don't be fooled by spots that look sunny when the leaves are off the trees at this time of year. Once those trees leaf out, a spot under their branches will be plunged in shade. Also, consider which sites would give your butterflies a little extra protection from the wind. For example, if the prevailing wind in your area is from the west, a site on the east side of a windbreak that runs north and south would be ideal.

If you already have a lilac growing in your yard, you may be able to plant this garden to one side of it so you don't have to buy another lilac. If you like, you can adapt my design and plant the other flowers around your lilac.

Buy Seeds, Plants, and Supplies

You can buy most of the seeds and plants for this garden at local garden centers or nurseries. You may not find Joe-Pye weed or a butterfly bush locally, but they are worth the extra trouble to order them by mail, especially once you see them covered with butterflies in the fall. See "Where to Buy" on this page for a list of companies that offer plants for this garden.

WHERE TO BUY

Buy the annual seeds and the lilac for this garden at your local garden center. Or, if you prefer, you can order seeds from one of the following companies:

- W. Atlee Burpee & Co., 300 Park Avenue, Warminster, PA 18974

- Park Seed Co., Cokesbury Road, Greenwood, SC 29647

- Stokes Seeds, Inc., P.O. Box 548, Buffalo, NY 14240-0548

You can order all the perennials from the following companies. André Viette Farm & Nursery also has an excellent selection of butterfly bushes.

- Holbrook Farm & Nursery, 115 Lance Road, P.O. Box 368, Fletcher, NC 28732

- André Viette Farm & Nursery, Route 1, Box 16, Fishersville, VA 22939

In addition to the seeds and plants, you will need the following supplies to plant this garden:

- Three 40-pound bags of compost or composted manure. Or substitute homemade compost—one full bin or three wheelbarrows full.

- One 5-pound bag of natural organic fertilizer

- One 25-foot soaker hose, ¾ inch in diameter

- Three large bags of shredded organic mulch, such as pine bark, cedar bark, or pine needles. Or substitute an equivalent amount of your own compost or a mix of compost and shredded leaves.

• One sturdy 6- to 8-foot trellis for the morning glories

SEASON TWO
(MARCH, APRIL, AND MAY)

Prepare the Site

Before you start preparing your garden site, make sure the soil is no longer frozen and that it is dry enough to dig without forming muddy clumps. See "Getting Ready to Plant" on page 42 for complete information on preparing the soil. (If you like, you can prepare the site for this garden in the fall and plant the following spring.)

Mark off an area that is 6 feet wide and 12 feet long with stakes and string or a sprinkling of lime or flour. Next, clear away rocks and debris, and use a sharp garden spade to remove any grass that is growing there. Use the grass you've removed to patch spots in your lawn or place it upside down on your compost pile. Spread the organic matter evenly over the site and dig the en-

tire garden to a depth of 8 inches either by hand or with a rotary tiller. Break up the clods to make a crumbly soil. Add half the bag of natural organic fertilizer and rake that into the top 2 to 4 inches of the soil. Rake the whole area smooth, and you are ready to plant.

Plant the Shrubs and Perennials

Plant the shrubs and perennials for this garden in early spring after the soil has thawed and is dry enough to dig without clumping up. (This is March in southern states and mid- to late April in northern ones.) When you are ready to plant, bring all the plants outdoors to the site you've prepared.

Before you plant anything, set the shrubs and perennials in place, following the garden design on page 148. First, decide where to plant the lilac or mock orange by drawing a 4-foot-diameter circle in the soil on the back left side of the garden using a trowel or stick. Then place the shrub you've chosen in the center of the circle. Draw a similar circle in the back right side of the garden and place the butterfly bush there.

Place the bee balm 1 foot in front of the lilac circle on the left side of the garden. Then place the butterfly weed in front of the bee balm in the front left corner of the garden.

The phlox, New England asters, and Joe-Pye weed go in a semicircle around the butterfly bush. Place the phlox 1 foot in front of the butterfly bush circle on the right side of the garden. Next, draw a 3-foot-diameter circle in the back row next to the butterfly bush, and put the Joe-Pye weed in that. The New England asters go between the Joe-Pye weed and the phlox. Finally, space out spread the purple coneflowers and 'Autumn Joy' sedum out across the center of the garden, leaving room for the cosmos seeds, which you'll plant a little later in the season. Place the gloriosa daisy slightly in front of the bee balm and sedum.

You can plant the parsley now, too, if you like, since it is quite cold-tolerant. It goes in the center of the garden in the very front.

Once you have placed each of the plants, step back and see if you like the arrangement. If they don't look right, feel free to move them around until they look good to you—after all, it's your garden. But make sure you check the sizes in the plant guide on page 150 before you actually plant—you don't want to put the tall plants in front of the short ones.

Plant all of the shrubs and perennials in the same way. Dig a hole wide enough to accommodate the roots of the plant comfortably. Place the plant deep enough in the hole so the crown of the plant, the place where the roots meet the stem, is at ground level. Gather soil around the base of the plant and press down firmly with your hands to eliminate any air pockets. Water each plant thoroughly after you have planted it. After that, water the whole garden once a week—less often if you receive ½ inch or more of rainfall.

Plant the Seeds

You can sow the seeds for your annual flowers once all danger of frost has passed in your area. (Depending on where you live, this can be any-time from March in the southern states to May in the northern ones.) You can always try to plant the seeds a little bit earlier than this, but until the ground is warm, they just won't germinate.

Before you sow any seeds, though, install the trellis by "planting" it at the back of your garden, as shown in the garden design on page 148. If your butterfly garden is up against a house or garage, screw it into the side of the building, no more than 1 foot off the ground.

Use a garden rake to break up the soil where you are going to plant your seeds. This helps break up any soil compaction and ensures that the soil will be loose enough for the new seedlings to send down roots. Then rake each site as smooth as possible.

Plant the morning glory seeds at the base of the trellis, the cosmos seeds next to the lilac and bee balm, and the Mexican sunflower seeds 1 foot or so in front of the morning glories. Then sow the zinnias, marigolds, and nasturtiums along the front of the garden, as shown in the design on page 148.

When you sow, try to scatter the seeds evenly, about 2 inches apart, in their respective locations. Cover the seeds with ½ inch of garden soil and press the area firmly with your hands so that the seeds will make good contact with the soil.

Water the seeded areas lightly every other day until new seedlings appear. Keep the baby plants watered until they are 3 to 4 inches tall. After that, you can reduce watering and care for them the same way as you would for established plants.

Add a Touch of Wilderness

Butterflies are wild creatures, so add a few extra touches to this garden

Butterflies like moist spots but can drown in deep water. Give them a shallow pan with water and a little bit of soil or pebbles in it.

to make them feel at home. They like to perch on logs, rest on warm sunny rocks, and gather around mud puddles to drink.

Find a couple of broken tree branches or pieces of firewood that are 2 to 3 feet long and place them in the garden. It doesn't matter where you put them as long as it doesn't interfere with the growth of the plants. Butterflies will use these as perches.

Next, create a butterfly sunbathing spot. Place a large flat rock or two in a sunny spot in the garden. (A couple of large round rocks will work also.) The stones warm up with the sun's rays and attract the butterflies.

Finally, create a little mud puddle for them by sinking an old birdbath, saucer, or plate up to its rim. Put a handful or two of soil in it. (If you don't want muddy water, use pebbles instead. But remember, butterflies love the minerals in mud.) Fill this butterfly bath with water once in a while if the rains don't keep it filled.

SEASON THREE (JUNE, JULY, AND AUGUST)

Minimize Chores and Enjoy Your Garden

Once your annuals are up and growing strongly, thin the marigolds, nasturtiums, and zinnias so they are 4 to 6 inches apart. Thin the cosmos and Mexican sunflowers so they are between 8 and 10 inches apart. You can either compost the thinnings or try to dig them up and plant them in some other garden.

After you have thinned your seedlings, snake your soaker hose through the garden, so it waters as much of the area as possible. Be sure to leave the connecting end visible so you can attach it to your conventional garden hose. Then pull up any weeds that might have sprouted while the garden was unmulched. Finally, spread a 2- to 4-inch layer of natural organic mulch over the soaker hose and the garden bed to stifle weeds and hold in moisture.

You won't have to water this garden as long as it rains at least

½ inch per week. The mulch will hold moisture in the soil and keep it cool and moist. Mulch also suppresses weeds, so it saves you watering and weeding time. When you do need to water, attach your garden hose to the soaker hose, then turn on the water and let it run for one to two hours, or until the soil in the garden is soaked to a depth of 6 inches. Don't water any more than once a week, but be sure to water thoroughly when you do.

As the morning glories grow, train them by gently moving their twining stems onto the trellis. If you like, you can also train them to crawl over onto your lilac.

Deadheading is important in a butterfly garden because it keeps your plants blooming—and that means a steady supply of food for your butterflies.

It is important to keep a steady supply of new flowers coming for your butterflies to feed on. To encourage your plants to keep blooming, remove faded flowers with a pinch of your fingers or a sharp pair of garden scissors.

SEASON FOUR (SEPTEMBER AND OCTOBER)

Prepare the Garden for Winter

As frost kills the annual plants, pull them up and toss them in the compost pile. Remove the soaker hose, drain it, and store it for the winter. Cut the perennials down to the ground after the ground is fully frozen, usually after Christmas in most years. After that, cover the garden with a 4-inch layer of shredded leaves, compost, or a combination of the two to protect the plants from the ravages of a cold dry winter.

You won't need to do anything to the lilac or mock orange for several years. Eventually, you may remove a dead branch or two, or thin out the center by removing an older stem. Do this sort of pruning in late winter.

BUTTERFLIES UP CLOSE AND PERSONAL

One of the best ways to enjoy your butterfly garden is to pull up a chair not far from it and simply sit and watch all the activity. Butterflies aren't shy once they're used to seeing you there, so you will be able to enjoy them up close.

It's also fun to identify the different kinds of butterflies that visit your garden and learn more about their habits. Look for a butterfly field guide at your local library. *Butterflies: How to Identify and Attract Them to Your Garden*, by Marcus Schneck, has color drawings of 250 common butterflies along with a range map for each and information about the plants that attract them.

Next spring, remove the mulch from the perennials as soon as they begin to poke their new shoots out. Leave the rest of the mulch in place. Then sprinkle 2 tablespoons of natural organic fertilizer around the base of each plant and work it into the soil with your fingers. Once warm weather arrives, you can plant annuals again and wait for the butterflies to return for another year.

Peek-Through Picket Fence Flowers

Perennials and Annuals to Perk Up a Fence

WALKING INTO a colorful, fragrant garden like this gives you that warm feeling you used to get in Grandma's garden. The exuberant blooms of cosmos, foxgloves, larkspurs, and sweet peas peek out from between the slats of a picket fence. A fragrant climbing rose clambers on an arbor over the front gate.

This design lets you add that old-fashioned appeal to your own yard with a long, narrow border of easy-to-grow flowers. Use this design to line your sidewalk with flowers and put a welcoming "face" on your house. Or plant it anywhere in your yard to dress up a fence.

4′ × 33′

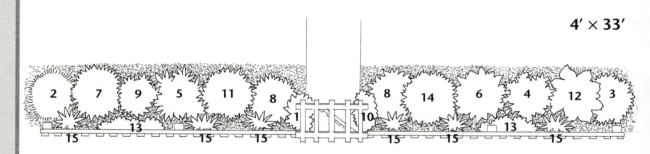

1. Clematis	6. Gas plant	11. Rocket larkspurs
2. Cleome	7. Goldenrod	12. Sunflowers
3. Cosmos	8. Love-lies-bleeding	13. Sweet peas
4. Delphinium	9. Lupine	14. Yarrow
5. Foxglove	10. 'New Dawn' rose	15. Daffodils

SEEDS TO BUY

Buy one packet of each of the following annuals:

- Cleome
- Cosmos
- Love-lies-bleeding
- Rocket larkspurs
- Sunflowers
- Sweet peas

Your whole neighborhood will enjoy the colorful flowers spilling through your picket fence.

PLANTS TO BUY

Buy one of each of the following plants:

- Clematis
- Delphinium
- Foxglove
- Gas plant
- Goldenrod
- Lupine
- 'New Dawn' rose
- Yarrow

BULBS TO BUY

Buy one or two dozen daffodil bulbs.

THE PLANT GUIDE

PLANTS FOR A PICKET FENCE GARDEN

THIS IS a long, thin mixed border that will provide you with colorful blooms from early spring until late fall. It features old-fashioned annuals, perennials, and bulbs, plus a climbing rose and clematis vine to cover an arbor with a profusion of colorful flowers.

Seeds

Buy one packet of each of the following annuals:

Cleome (*Cleome hasslerana*). Also called spider flower, cleome's tall arching flower stems in pink, purple, and white will tower over a fence. This delicate-looking but dramatic plant reaches 4 to 5 feet tall by the end of the summer. The spidery-looking flowers appear along the central stalk from early summer to fall. Cleome is an annual that will reseed.

Cosmos (*Cosmos* spp.). One of the easiest of all annuals to grow, cosmos bears daisylike flowers in many different colors. For this design, garden cosmos (*C. bipinnatus*) is best. Look for taller types that reach 3 to 4 feet at least. 'Sensation' series cultivars in pink, red, and white are ideal.

Love-lies-bleeding (*Amaranthus caudatus*). This odd-looking annual plant has some very colorful common names, but my favorite is kiss-me-over-the-garden-gate, which seems especially appropriate for this garden. It's a dramatic-looking plant that produces blood red, ropelike tassels of flowers that look more like seedheads than anything else. Plants can reach about 2 feet in height.

Rocket larkspur (*Consolida ambigua*). Larkspurs resemble delphiniums, but they are easier to grow. (They're sometimes sold as *Delphinium ajacis*.) Flowers appear in fluffy-looking, 4-foot spikes in purple, lavender, blue, pink, and white. These are annuals that will reseed if you find a site they like. 'Giant Imperial' is an especially nice mix.

Sunflowers (*Helianthus annuus*). Although giant sunflowers would tower over even formidable fences, for this garden, try one of the new 4- to 5-foot ornamental sunflowers. They make great cutting and border plants, with flowers in lemon, orange, mahogany, or white. Some good ones to look for include yellow 'Moonwalker', which bears branched flowerstalks, lemon-yellow 'Valentine', or creamy yellow 'Italian White'.

Sweet peas (*Lathyrus odoratus*). Sweet peas are old-fashioned annuals that love cool spring weather. For this garden, be sure to get climbing sweet peas, not dwarf ones. Blooms come in peach, white, lavender-blue, purple, and rose and appear in late spring and early summer. The vining plants reach 4 to 6 feet. If you live in an area where springs can get warm, look for heat-resistant types.

Plants

Buy one of each of the following perennials:

Delphiniums (*Delphinium* spp.). These old-fashioned perennials pro-

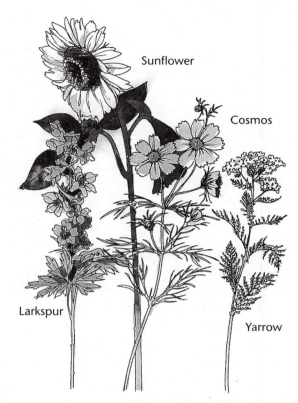

Most of the plants in this garden have long stems and make excellent cut flowers. Be sure to bring some indoors to enjoy, take them to work, or share them with neighbors or shut-ins.

duce dense spikes of blue, purple, rose, or white flowers that look beautiful peeking over a picket fence. They tend to be short-lived in areas where summers are warm, though, and are often grown as annuals for that reason. Plants bloom in early summer on 2- to 5-foot stems, depending on the cultivar you choose. Choose one plant of any hybrid that appeals to you. 'Blue Fountains' is heat-resistant. Zones 3 or 4 to 8.

Foxglove (*Digitalis purpurea*). Foxglove is actually a biennial that self-sows so freely that you'd think it was a perennial. In summer, it produces 3-foot spikes with bell-shaped flowers in purple, red, pink, and white. Zones 4 to 8.

Gas plant (*Dictamnus albus*). Gas plant is such an unfortunate name for a great perennial. The name refers to the fact that the flowers are so fragrant that they emit a flammable, lemon-scented oil. Even the foliage of this plant is lemon-scented. Gas plant bears tall spikes of flowers that range from 1 to 4 feet. As the name *albus* implies, gas plant has white flowers, but the cultivar 'Purpureus' has pink flowers. The plants grow 1 to 4 feet tall and bloom in early summer. Zones 3 to 8.

Goldenrods (*Solidago* spp.). Contrary to popular opinion, goldenrods do not cause hay fever and other allergies. They make a wonderful addition to any garden, where their golden yellow blooms add much-needed color in the fall. You may have to look around a bit to find plants, but it's well worth the effort. Mail-order perennial nurseries often carry goldenrods. Species goldenrods like Canada goldenrod (*S. canadensis*) and stiff goldenrod (*S. rigida*) are available from wildflower nurseries. Herb specialists offer goldenrods, too, including sweet goldenrod (*S. odora*), which has anise-scented leaves. Plants reach 3 to 5 feet at maturity. Zones 3 to 9, depending on the species you buy.

Lupines (*Lupinus* spp.). Lupines produce stately flowerstalks packed with pea-shaped blooms in pink, blue, red, white, or bicolors. The plants reach 3 to 4 feet and bloom in early summer. Zones 3 to 7.

Yarrows (*Achillea* spp.). Ferny foliage, colorful flat-topped flowers and an easy-to-please disposition make these plants classic perennials. Plants are drought-tolerant and bear white, yellow, salmon, brick-red, or pink flowers on 2- to 3-foot stems in late spring and summer. Look for 'Coronation Gold', 'Moonshine', or one of the new Galaxy series cultivars. Zones 3 to 8.

Climbing Plants

There's nothing more romantic-looking than a gate with a rose-covered arbor over it. If you have an arbor over your gate, I suggest you buy a rose and a clematis plant to cover it. And if you don't have an arbor, why not add one?

'New Dawn' rose (*Rosa* 'New Dawn'). This is a disease-resistant, hardy climbing rose that produces lovely cameo pink flowers in profusion in early summer and then continues to bloom on and off for the rest of the season. The canes can reach 15 feet or more. Buy one bush to plant on your arbor over a gate, if you have one. Zones 5 to 9.

Clematis (*Clematis* spp.). Clematis is a hardy, vigorous perennial vine that you should buy to plant on the other side of your arbor. Once established, it will grow over the top of the arbor and entwine with the 'New Dawn' rose. I suggest white-flowered 'Marie Boisselot', ruby red 'Niobe', or heavy-blooming pink 'Hagley Hybrid'. All are vigorous, heavy-blooming plants that will cover your arbor with color when the rose is blooming only sporadically. If you don't have an arbor over the gate, you may want to put the clematis somewhere else. Clematis is hardy from Zones 3 or 4 to 9, depending on the cultivar you choose.

Bulbs

Daffodils (*Narcissus* spp.). There is nothing quite like the sight of daf-fodils sticking their sunny little faces out between the slats of a picket fence, so be sure to save room for some. They'll begin the bloom parade in early spring. There are hundreds of daffodils to choose from. Look at your local garden center or in mail-order catalogs and pick your favorites. To extend the season even further, buy a variety of cultivars that bloom in early, mid-, and late spring. A dozen or two bulbs should be enough for planting your first year.

Careful picking can mean big dividends when you select daffodils. For a few cents more per bulb, you can buy triple-nosed bulbs. You'll see the benefits in your garden—each "nose" will flower either next spring or the one after. Single-nosed bulbs will take a few years to bloom as much.

THE SEASONAL GUIDE

SEASON ONE (JANUARY AND FEBRUARY)

Select a Site

If you already have a picket fence, you really don't need to spend any time scouting for a site for this garden. Just make sure your site is in full sun. The plants in this garden need at least six hours of direct sunshine a day to bloom their best, even though some of them will tolerate light shade.

If you don't have a picket fence but would like to add one to your yard, why not look over your options and select a style now? See page 171 for some attractive fence styles.

You will plant this garden in three stages. Plant the cold-hardy perennials and cool-season annuals in early spring; plant tender annuals in late spring after the danger of frost is past. You'll buy and plant the daffodil bulbs in the fall.

Buy the Seeds, Plants, and Supplies

You probably don't need to look any farther than your local garden center for the old-fashioned flowers in this garden. If you would like a wider range of choices, though, see "Where to Buy" on the opposite page for some suggestions of mail-order companies. In many cases, local seed racks only offer seed packets of mixed colors, but by mail you can often buy the specific colors you want. For example, Shepherd's Garden Seeds offers packets of pink and blue florist-quality larkspurs in addition to packets of mixed-color seed.

If your garden is located in warmer climates anywhere south of a line drawn from New York to Chicago, you should have a growing season long enough to plant all of your annual seeds directly in the garden and get great blooms in mid-summer. North of that, you will probably need to start seed for love-lies-bleeding, which takes a while to get growing, indoors.

In addition to the plants listed for this garden, you'll need the following supplies:

• Three 40-pound bags of compost or composted manure. Or substitute homemade compost—one full bin or three wheelbarrows full.

• One 5-pound bag of natural organic fertilizer

• Two 4-cubic-foot bags of additional organic matter, such as compost, chopped leaves, or rotted sawdust

• One or two 25-foot soaker hoses, ¾ inch in diameter (optional)

• Four large bags of shredded organic mulch, such as pine bark, cedar bark, or pine needles. Or substitute an equivalent amount of your own compost or a mix of compost and shredded leaves.

SEASON TWO
(MARCH, APRIL, AND MAY)

Start Seeds Indoors

If you live in the North or just want to give your slow-growing love-lies-bleeding plants an extra-early start, sow them indoors. Don't worry—

WHERE TO BUY

You can order the perennials, clematis, rose, and bulbs from any of the following sources:

• Park Seed Company, Cokesbury Road, Greenwood, SC 29647

• W. Atlee Burpee and Co., 300 Park Avenue, Warminster, PA 18974

• White Flower Farm, P.O. Box 50, Litchfield, CT 06759-0050

For an excellent selection of seeds, write Park, Burpee, or either of the following companies:

• Shepherd's Garden Seeds, 30 Irene Street, Torrington, CT 06790

• Thompson & Morgan, Inc., P.O. Box 1308, Jackson, NJ 08527

---

they're *easy* to grow indoors. Plan to sow the seed five to six weeks before the last frost date for your area. If you don't know what that date is, call your local Cooperative Extension Service office (listed under city or county government in your telephone book) or a local garden center and ask them.

To start your seeds, buy cell packs or eight to ten peat pots and a bag of commercial seed-starting mix. (Or, if you like, you can buy a seed-starting kit at your local garden center.) Fill the cells or peat pots nearly to the top with seed-starting mix and gently pat the soil mix down. Then water thoroughly until the soil is completely wet. (You may want to water the night before you are ready to sow and let the soil mix soak up the water overnight.) Sprinkle two or three seeds in each cell or pot and lightly cover with $1/16$ inch of soil. Tamp down lightly and cover your pots with plastic wrap to increase humidity.

Place the newly sown seeds in a warm place (between 70° and 75°F) and mist them with water daily until they germinate. They don't need a sunny spot until they have germinated, but when they do, move them to a sunny window.

When the seedlings are about 2 inches tall and have at least one set of true leaves, use a small pair of scissors to snip out all but the healthiest-looking seedling per cell or pot.

Two weeks before you plan to put your love-lies-bleeding plants in the garden, take them outside to a protected, partially shaded spot during the day to get them acclimated to the outdoors. Start by bringing them out for an hour or so, and gradually increase the time they spend outdoors so they can get used to outdoor conditions. Leave them out overnight during the last few days before planting time. Be sure to bring them in at night if frost threatens.

Prepare the Site

You can prepare the site for this garden in the fall and plant it the following spring, or prepare it in spring a few weeks before you are ready to plant. See "Getting Ready to Plant" on page 42 for complete information on preparing the soil. If you don't already have a low fence along the site you have selected, now is the time to install one.

To prepare the site, clear two beds, each 4 feet deep and 15 feet wide, on either side of your gate, as shown in the garden design on page 162. Slice off the grass with a sharp spade and use it to patch spots in your lawn or place it upside down on your compost pile. Then remove any rocks, brush, or other weedy growth and discard or place it in your compost bin.

Spread the organic matter and the fertilizer over the entire garden area and dig the soil to a depth of 6 to 8 inches. You can dig the soil by hand or till it with a rotary tiller as long as you can reach into the corners without tearing up the fence. To protect the fence, dig along it with a garden fork. Be sure to break up any clumps. After you've finished digging, rake the area smooth, and you are ready to plant.

EXPRESS YOURSELF WITH PICKETS

If you don't already have a fence for your flowers to peek through, selecting one can be great fun. As you can see from the picket fence styles shown here, all picket fences aren't the same. Look around and see what ready-made styles are available in your area. If you are handy, you can build your own picket fence from patterns in a woodworking book. *A Country Garden for Your Backyard* by Marny Smith and Nancy DuBrule has complete directions for four styles of fences. You can paint your fence the traditional white, or choose a color that will complement your house.

This garden would also look lovely with a more rustic split-rail fence. Or, if you enjoy the Victorian look of cast iron and enjoy shopping for old treasures, perhaps you could find sections of an old cast-iron fence at an antique market.

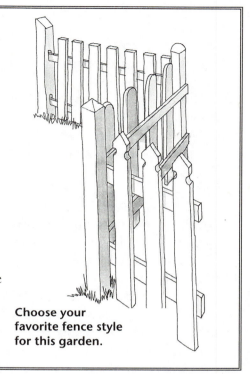

Choose your favorite fence style for this garden.

Plant Perennials, Vines, and Cold-Hardy Annuals

Sow the larkspur and sweet pea seeds as soon as the ground is thawed and you can work in it without making muddy clumps. This can be as early as late February in warmer areas and late March to early April in cooler climates. The day before you are ready to plant, soak the sweet-pea seeds in warm water overnight to speed their germination.

To plant the larkspur seeds, rake the soil smooth in the area where larkspur is supposed to go, as shown on the garden design on page 162. Be sure to leave room for the love-lies-bleeding and clematis between the larkspurs and the gate. Sprinkle the seeds evenly over the area, spacing them about 4 to 6 inches apart. Cover with ½ inch of soil, press down lightly with your hands, and water. Keep the soil evenly moist until the seeds germinate.

Plant the sweet peas at the base of the fence on both sides of the gate, as shown in the garden design. To plant them, rake a 3-foot-long strip smooth.

Then dig a 1-inch-deep trench at the base of the fence. Place the peas in the trench about 2 inches apart. Cover with soil, press down with your hands, and water. Keep the soil evenly moist until the seeds germinate.

About two or three weeks after you plant the larkspur and the sweet-pea seeds, the weather should have warmed up a bit and you can set out the clematis, delphinium, foxglove, gas plant, goldenrod, lupine, rose-bush, and yarrow. If you are planting a bareroot rosebush, soak it in a bucket of water the night before you are ready to plant. Then carry the rose in the bucket of water to the garden so it doesn't dry out before you plant it. (For information on handling roses, see "Plant the Garden" on page 128 in the chapter on roses.)

When you are ready to plant, take all your plants out to the garden and place them where you plan to plant them. Again, follow the garden design on page 162 for the exact locations.

Plant all of the perennials and the clematis in the same way. Dig a hole that is larger and deeper than the root ball of the plant you are planting. Since you have just recently prepared the garden bed, the soil should be loose and easy to work. Place the plant into the hole so that the roots fit comfortably and aren't crowded. Be sure to set the plant at the same depth it was in the pot. The crown of the plant, where the root zone meets the main stem of the plant, should be at ground level. Gather soil into the hole and around the stem and press down firmly with your hands. Water deeply so the soil is soaked around the plant.

Bareroot roses look scary, with their stubby tops and tangle of roots, but they are very easy to grow as long as you handle them properly at planting time. Be sure to read and follow the rose planting directions on page 128 that I mentioned above. You will find instructions on training your rose to grow on its trellis on page 131.

Keep all of your newly planted plants watered—every few days is best, if you don't have ample rain—at least until the plants have recovered and are growing strongly. Keeping up with watering makes a big difference in getting them established.

Plant the Heat-Loving Annuals

As soon as there is no longer any threat of frost in your area, you can plant all the rest of the annuals—the love-lies-bleeding plants and the cleome, cosmos, and sunflower seeds.

Plant two or three love-lies-bleeding seedlings spaced 12 to 16 inches apart on each side of the garden gate. Don't be fooled by their small size now. They will get really big by late summer. To plant, dig a hole large enough to fit the root ball comfortably. Plant the transplants so they are at the same depth or slightly deeper than they were in the pots. Refill the hole with soil, press down firmly with your hands, and water.

To sow the cleome, cosmos, and sunflower seeds, use a rake and loosen and smooth the soil on the areas where they are to grow. Each gets an oval site that is about 2 feet wide and as deep as the planting bed. Sprinkle the cleome and cosmos seeds over the areas so the seeds are approximately 4 inches apart. Cover the seeds with ¼ inch of fine soil and press down lightly with your hands. Scatter the sunflower seeds over their site, spacing them 6 inches apart. Poke the seeds into the soil about ½ inch deep, fill the tiny holes with soil, and press down firmly with your hands. Water well.

SEASON THREE
(JUNE, JULY, AND AUGUST)

Minimize Chores and Enjoy Your Garden

About two to four weeks after you have planted the seeds, begin thinning them out so the remaining seedlings stand about 8 inches apart. When you thin, carefully pinch the plants off by hand or snip them off at ground level with a sharp knife or garden scissors.

Once the clematis begins growing, take a minute or two to train its tendrils onto the trellis. All you need to do is loop them around one of the slats and they'll do the rest.

It isn't an easy matter to install a soaker hose in this garden. You can't just run it down the center because visitors will trip over it when they come through the gate. If you like, you can loop separate soaker hoses through each end of the garden and cover them with mulch. Be sure to leave the connecting ends where you will be able to reach them. Some soaker hoses have kits that allow you to divide your hose in half and attach it to nonporous PVC pipe, which you can run under the walkway in the center of the garden. But this isn't really feasible unless you have a mulched path into which you can sink the pipe.

If you don't install a soaker hose, I suggest you water this garden by screwing an adjustable bronze nozzle onto your conventional garden hose, set the nozzle on mist, and place it in the garden for one hour, not more often than once a week, moving the nozzle to a different spot every ten minutes until you have soaked the entire garden bed.

Whether you install a soaker hose or not, apply a 2- to 4-inch layer of natural organic mulch. Organic mulch stifles weeds, keeps the soil cooler and evenly moist, and also adds organic matter to the soil as it decomposes. It also makes your garden look quite nice. Compost is an excellent mulch and so is shredded bark. Use whatever mulch you like, or better yet, use a combination of compost or shredded leaves and bark.

Throughout the summer, be sure to pick flowers from this garden for bouquets. Cut the dead stalks off of the lupine and delphinium after they have bloomed. If you are lucky, the delphinium may bloom again.

Season Four (September and October)

Plant the Daffodil Bulbs

September and early October are the best months of the year to plant daffodil bulbs. You'll find that garden centers start offering them at that time, and bulb catalogs begin arriving in your mailbox around Labor Day.

I suggest you plant three clumps of daffodils on each side of the garden. Bring the bulbs out to the garden and place them 4 inches apart in their clusters just beneath or close to the picket fence. Dig holes 8 to 10 inches deep and place the bulbs in the holes pointed ends up. Fill the holes and press down the soil. That's all there is to it.

Prepare the Garden for Winter

As cold weather kills the cleome, cosmos, larkspur, love-lies-bleeding, and sunflowers, pull them up from the garden and toss them in the compost bin. (In most areas, the sweet peas will succumb once hot weather arrives, since they are really cool-season annuals.)

When the really cold weather arrives and the ground freezes, cut the delphinium, foxglove, gas plant, goldenrod, lupine, and yarrow to within 1 to 2 inches of the ground and toss the remains in the compost bin. Leave the clematis and the rose alone. Remove the soaker hoses, if you used them. Drain and store them for the winter.

Cover the entire garden with a blanket of straw, compost, shredded leaves, or pine boughs to protect it from the harsh winter. A good blanket of snow is just as beneficial. Remove the mulch in the spring when the weather warms up and the perennials begin to send up their early sprouts.

Hollyhocks, Phlox, and Four-o'Clocks

An Old-Fashioned Garden

THERE'S NO DENYING the charm of old-fashioned flowers. They generally come in classic shapes and colors, are beautiful for bouquets, and bloom cheerfully in a wide range of conditions. Best of all for beginning gardeners, they are easy to grow.

This is a planting with flowers that hold special memories. Perhaps your grandmother or great aunt once lovingly tended her favorite peonies, daisies, or phlox— just like the ones in this design. Single hollyhocks, like the ones in the back row of this design, may remind you of a cottage garden or a planting against a country barn.

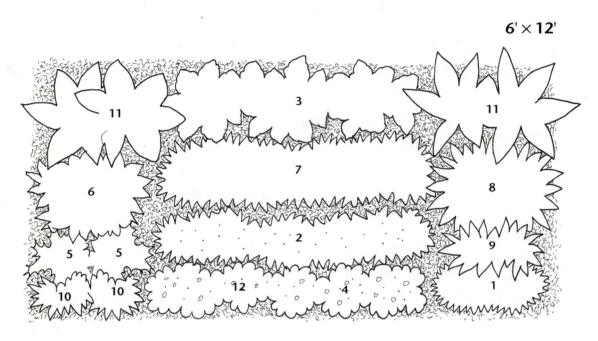

6' × 12'

1. Cottage pinks
2. Four-o'clocks
3. Hollyhocks
4. Nasturtiums
5. Oriental poppies
6. Peony
7. Phlox
8. Shasta daisy
9. Sundrops
10. Sweet Williams
11. Cannas
12. Daffodils

You'll get loads of blooms all season from your hollyhocks, phlox, and four-o'clocks garden.

SEEDS TO BUY

Buy one packet of each of the following plants:

- Four-o'clocks
- Nasturtiums

BULBS TO BUY

- Cannas. Buy four rhizomes or plants.
- Daffodils. Buy two dozen bulbs.

PLANTS TO BUY

Buy one of each of the following perennials, unless otherwise noted:

- Cottage pinks. Buy two.
- Hollyhocks. Buy five or six.
- Oriental poppies. Buy two.
- Peony
- Phlox. Buy three.
- Shasta daisy
- Sundrops
- Sweet Williams. Buy two or three.

THE PLANT GUIDE

PLANTS FOR AN OLD-FASHIONED GARDEN

OLD-FASHIONED flowers hold a special place in my heart. I have inherited plantings of hollyhocks, peonies, Shasta daisies, and other old-fashioned flowers in various homes throughout my life. Over the years, I have grown to appreciate their simple charm and carefree ways, and I am sure you will, too. This design is a mixture of perennials, annuals, and bulbs that will give you years of pleasure.

Seeds

Buy one packet of each of the following plants:

Four-o'clocks (*Mirabilis jalapa*). These easy-to-grow, old-time favorites produce fragrant, multicolored blossoms that open at about four o'clock on warm summer afternoons. Also called "marvel of Peru" for their opening show, these bushy annuals reach about 3 feet and bloom from July until frost.

Nasturtiums (*Tropaeolum majus*). These colorful annuals tolerate drought and poor soil, yet cover themselves with colorful red, orange, or yellow blooms all summer. The leaves and flowers are peppery-tasting—they're great when added to salads. For this garden, buy either 'Alaska', which has beautiful green leaves variegated with white, or plants in the Jewel series. Both grow 8 to 12 inches tall.

Plants

Buy one of each of the following plants, unless otherwise noted:

Cottage pinks (*Dianthus plumarius*). Old-fashioned cottage pinks make great additions to any garden. They have attractive blue-green foliage that's evergreen, and they produce small, fragrant five-petaled flowers with edges that look like they were cut with pinking shears. Flowers come three to five per stem and are pink or white. Plants are from 1½ to 2 feet tall. If you like, you can substitute maiden pinks (*D. deltoides*) or cheddar pinks (*D. gratianopolitanus*). Buy two plants. Zones 3 to 9.

Hollyhocks (*Alcea rosea*). No old-fashioned garden would be complete without these tall biennials with their spikes of saucerlike blooms. For this garden, buy the old-fashioned single types, not the modern ruffled doubles. Hollyhocks will reseed themselves so easily you will come to think of them as perennials. Plants reach 5 to 7 feet. Buy five or six plants from your local garden center. Zones 3 to 8.

Oriental poppy (*Papaver orientale*). The orange-red blooms of oriental poppies have been popular with gardeners for generations. They appear soon after spring bulbs have faded. There are many new oriental poppies to choose from, including deep red-, white- and pink-flowered ones. The plants go dormant after blooming in early summer. Buy two plants for fall planting. Zones 2 to 7.

Peony (*Paeonia lactiflora*). What garden should be without at least one clump of glorious, late-spring –blooming peonies? Peonies are gen-

Hollyhocks

Sundrops

Cottage pinks   Shasta daisy

Old-fashioned flowers like these make beautiful, informal bouquets.

erally available for sale in the fall and are sold bareroot. Although you may see potted peonies for sale, you'll get the most for your money if you buy three- to five-eye (peony buds are called "eyes") bareroot divisions. Healthy, three- to five-eye divisions will bloom sooner than smaller one- to two-eye plants, too, which are sometimes potted up for sale. For this garden, you may want to look for one of the old-fashioned peonies, such as white-flowered 'Festiva Maxima' or pink 'Sarah Bernhardt', or simply select one that appeals to you. You'll find peonies with single and double blooms in white, pink, and red. Look around and buy one plant that appeals to you. Zones 3 to 8.

Phlox (*Phlox paniculata*, sometimes sold as *P. decussata*). Garden phlox is a classic, summer-blooming perennial that's a must for this garden. Plants bear domed clusters of white, pink, lilac, or magenta flowers on 2- to 3-foot plants. Look for mildew-resistant cultivars, including 'Bright Eyes', 'David', 'Eva Cullum', and 'Franz Schubert'. Buy three plants. Zones 3 or 4 to 8, depending on the cultivar you choose.

Shasta daisy (*Chrysanthemum × superbum*, also sold as *Leucanthemum × superbum*). This beloved garden perennial bears white-petaled daisies with gold button centers in early summer. Plants range from 1 to 3 feet tall. For this garden, look for one of the taller types—'Aglaya', 'Alaska', and 'Mount Shasta' are all good choices. Zones 4 to 8; 'Alaska' is hardy to Zone 3.

Sundrops (*Oenothera fruticosa* or *O. tetragona*). Not surprisingly, sundrops bear sunny, bright yellow clusters of flowers that will add appeal to any garden. Choose either of the species listed above—both are between 2 and 3 feet tall, bloom throughout the summer, and open their flowers during the day. (Other members of this genus are commonly called evening primroses because their flowers open in the afternoon or evening.) *O. fruticosa* is hardy in Zones 4 to 8; *O. tetragona*, Zones 3 to 8.

Sweet William (*Dianthus barbatus*). Hardy, old-fashioned sweet William is actually a biennial, but since it self-sows freely, it behaves like a perennial. Plants produce dense round heads of bicolored flowers in pink, red, and white and are 10 to 12 inches tall. This plant is easy from seed, too. Buy two or three plants. Zones 3 to 9.

Bulbs

This garden features daffodils, which are true bulbs, as well as cannas, which are actually grown from fleshy rhizomes.

Daffodils (*Narcissus* spp.). There are hundreds of daffodils to choose from. Look at your local garden center or in mail-order catalogs and pick your favorites. When you buy, spend a little more to get the larger, better-quality bulbs rather than the super-cheap assortments. (For more on buying quality bulbs, see the illustration on page 167.) Buy two dozen bulbs. Zones 4 to 9, depending on the species and cultivar you select.

Canna (*Canna × generalis*). Canna, sometimes called canna lily, is a bold plant often found in old-fashioned gardens. The plant features large, tropical-looking leaves and large clusters of pink, red, orange, or yellow flowers from midsummer to frost. Some cannas even have yellow-striped leaves. It needs compost-rich soil that is moist but well drained to grow well. A layer of mulch, applied after the plants are about 1 foot tall, helps hold moisture in the soil and increases soil organic matter. Since canna is a tender perennial, it is grown as an annual north of Zone 7. In areas where it is not hardy, plant the rhizomes outdoors in the spring after all danger of frost has passed. In the fall, dig and overwinter the rhizomes indoors the same way you would dahlia tubers. Plants range from 3 to 6 feet tall, depending on cultivar you choose. For this garden, look for a taller type, at least 3 feet tall. Buy four plants. Zones 7 to 10.

THE SEASONAL GUIDE

SEASON ONE (JANUARY AND FEBRUARY)

Select a Site

Take some time during the winter months to scout out a site for this garden. All the flowers in it need full sun to bloom their best. I think this old-fashioned garden is especially pretty planted against a fence, wall, or shed. A south- or east-facing site will give them the sun they need.

Buy Seeds, Plants, Bulbs, and Supplies

You probably can buy many or all of the seeds and plants for this garden at local garden centers and nurseries. But you may find a better selection of old-fashioned plants in some of the catalogs listed in "Where to Buy" on this page.

Keep in mind as you shop that most of the plants in this garden can be planted in late spring or early summer, but the daffodils, oriental poppies, and peony should be planted in the fall.

In addition to the seeds and plants listed for this garden, you'll need the following supplies:

• Three 40-pound bags of compost or composted manure. Or substitute homemade compost—one full bin or three wheelbarrows full.

• One 5-pound bag of natural organic fertilizer

• One 25-foot soaker hose, ¾ inch in diameter

• Four large bags of shredded organic mulch, such as pine bark, cedar bark, or pine needles. Or substitute an equivalent amount of your own compost or a mix of compost and shredded leaves.

Give the Cannas a Head Start

About a month before the last frost date in your area, if you've bought or ordered canna rhizomes, plant the canna rhizomes horizontally in pots with the buds pointing up. Cover them with about 1 inch of potting medium, and keep them warm and moist but not too wet until they sprout. Once they have

---

WHERE TO BUY

You can find these cheerful old-fashioned favorites at most garden centers, but you can often choose from a larger selection if you order by mail. Some catalogs list hundreds of daffodils! If you would like to order by mail, write for a catalog from one of the following companies:

• W. Atlee Burpee & Co., 300 Park Avenue, Warminster, PA 18974

• Wayside Gardens, 1 Garden Lane, Hodges, SC 29695-0001

• White Flower Farm, P.O. Box 50, Litchfield, CT 06759-0050

For an excellent selection of daffodils and cannas, try The Daffodil Mart, Route 3, Box 794, Gloucester, VA 23061. (Ask for their spring bulb catalog for daffodils and their summer bulb catalog for cannas.)

sprouted, keep them in a sunny place until you are ready to plant them outside. An alternative, if your local garden center carries cannas in containers, is to simply buy the plants and plant them in spring with your other perennials.

SEASON TWO (MARCH, APRIL, AND MAY)

Prepare the Site

This garden is 6 feet deep and 12 feet long. Before you begin preparing the site you have selected, check to make sure it will receive at least six full hours of direct sunlight during the middle of the day.

You actually have two options for improving the soil and planting this garden. You can improve the soil and plant everything but the peony, oriental poppies, and hardy bulbs in mid-spring or early summer as soon as the ground is warm and easy to work with a rotary tiller or garden spade. Or you can spend time during the summer improving the soil, and plant all the perennials in September. You can also sow hollyhock seed outdoors at that time.

To prepare for late spring or early summer planting, select a day when the soil is warm and you can dig it without forming muddy clumps. (See "Getting Your Garden Ready to Plant" on page 42 for complete information on preparing the soil.) First, mark off your site with short stakes so you don't lose track of its dimensions. Then clear away rocks and debris. Use a sharp spade to remove any grass that is growing there. Use the grass you've removed to patch spots in your lawn, or place it upside down on your compost pile.

Spread the compost and the fertilizer over this area. Then dig the soil to a depth of 8 inches using a rotary tiller or a garden fork. Be sure to break up as many clumps as possible, then rake the area smooth, and you are ready to plant.

Plant the Garden

You can plant all the plants in this garden, except the daffodils, oriental poppies, and peony, in spring after all danger of frost has passed in your area. If you started cannas indoors, start hardening them off—bringing them outdoors to a protected, partially shaded site to allow them to become acclimated to the outdoors—about two to three weeks before you are ready to plant. Start by bringing them out for an hour or so, and gradually increase the time they spend outdoors so they can get used to outdoor conditions. Leave them out overnight during the last few days before planting time.

Take the nasturtium and four-o'clock seeds, the cannas, and all the spring-planted perennials out to the garden. If you have a choice, plant your garden on an overcast, windless day to minimize sunscald and transplant shock. If it's not overcast, plant late in the day when the sun is going down and the plants can rest during the cool of the night.

Before you plant anything, set each plant in position and mark planting sites in the soil for the nasturtiums and four-o'clocks. Use the garden design on page 176 as a guide. You will see that the hollyhocks, phlox, and four-o'clocks take up the most room in this garden. Eventually, they will create a stairstep arrangement, with the tallest plants in the rear and shortest in front. Before you plant anything, step back and make sure you like the arrangement. Be sure to leave enough room for the oriental poppies and peony.

Plant the cannas, cottage pinks, hollyhocks, phlox, Shasta daisy, sundrops, and sweet Williams in the same manner. Dig a hole that is larger and deeper than the root ball of the plant you are planting. Since you have just recently prepared the garden bed, the soil should be loose and easy to work. Place the plant into the hole so that the roots fit comfortably and aren't crowded. Be sure to set the plant at the same depth that it was in the pot. The crown of the plant, where the root zone meets the main stem of the plant, should be at ground level. Gather soil into the hole and around the stem and press down firmly with your hands. Water deeply so the soil is soaked around the plant.

Next, sow the nasturtiums and four-o'clocks. Scatter the seeds over the surface of their planting area, spacing the nasturtiums 4 to 6 inches apart and the four-o'clocks 8 to 10 inches apart. Poke the seeds about 1/2 inch into the soil. Cover the seeds with soil, press down firmly with your hands, and water thoroughly. It is very important that you keep the seeded areas lightly moist until they germinate. Water them lightly every day until you see the seedlings emerge.

It's also important to keep the plants well watered while they are getting established. Water them thoroughly at least once a week for the first two to three weeks to be sure they have plenty of water.

SEASON THREE
(JUNE, JULY, AND AUGUST)

Minimize Chores and Enjoy Your Garden

About two to four weeks after you planted the seeds, check to make sure you spread the seed far enough apart when you planted it. If not, thin out the weakest seedlings so that the remaining plants will have room to grow. When you thin, carefully pinch the plants off by hand or snip them off at ground level with garden scissors.

Once your seedlings are up, install the soaker hose by snaking it through the garden, covering as much of the area as possible. Be careful to leave the connecting end visible. (Be sure to place it by all the cannas, which appreciate extra summer moisture.) After that, cover the soaker hose and the rest of the garden with a 2- to 4-inch-thick layer of natural organic mulch. This mulch will stifle weeds, keep moisture in the soil, and keep the soil cool. Spread mulch up to, but not touching, plant stems—otherwise it can cause rot.

SEASON FOUR
(SEPTEMBER AND OCTOBER)

Plant the Daffodils, Peony, and Poppies

Once fall arrives, it's time to plant the daffodils, peony, and oriental poppies. To plant the daffodils, simply push aside the still-blooming nasturtiums and plant the daffodils between them. The daffodils will be prettiest if you don't plant a ramrod-straight row of them. Instead, arrange them in clusters of three to five bulbs 4 inches apart, in holes 8 to 10 inches deep. Place the bulbs in the hole root end down, and cover them with soil.

To plant the peony, dig a hole wide enough and deep enough to accommodate the root system. (If you are planting bareroot divisions, don't be surprised if they are odd-looking. They look something like a shrub that has fleshy roots and the top cut off.) When you plant, be sure the pink "eyes" on the roots will be no more than 2 inches below the soil surface when your peony is finally settled in the soil. (For more on how to plant a peony, see the illustration on page 105.) Peonies that are planted too deeply won't bloom, so after you cover the roots with soil, double-check the depth of the eyes.

DAFFODIL COMPANIONS

After your daffodils stop flowering, it is tempting to cut off the leaves or at least tie them up so you won't have to look at them. But they are busy making food to fuel next year's flowers, so you need to leave them alone. This garden features one of the easiest ways to cope with ripening (a euphemistic gardening term for yellowing and dying) bulb foliage—cover it up with annuals.

Each spring, shortly after the daffodils have finished blooming, sow the site with nasturtiums, making sure you don't disturb the bulbs. The nasturtiums will fill the bed with flowers fast and keep it looking nice all summer. This trick will work with any shallow-rooted annuals, including impatiens, marigolds, petunias, and zinnias. You can tuck small bedding plants of these annuals in and around the bulbs.

Then gently tamp down the soil, and water well.

To plant the oriental poppies, dig a hole deep enough to accommodate the rather long taproot so that the crown of the plant is 1 to 2 inches below soil level. The roots are brittle, so handle them with care as you settle them into the soil. Then fill the hole with soil, firm it down with your hands, and water.

Water the peony and poppies once a week until cold weather arrives to make sure they start growing roots and become established.

Prepare the Garden for Winter

As cold weather approaches, frost will kill the tops of the cannas. When that happens, dig up the clumps, cut off the tops, and let the rhizomes dry in a warm dry place for a week. Shake off any excess soil and store them in a cool dry place for the winter.

As the nasturtiums and four-o'clocks are killed by frost, pull them up from the ground, and toss them in the compost bin. Remove the soaker hose, drain it, and store it for the winter.

Once the really cold weather arrives and the soil begins to freeze, cut the hollyhocks, phlox, and sundrops to ground level. Cover the entire garden with a 2- to 4-inch layer of shredded leaves, pine boughs, or straw to protect it from the freezing and thawing that's a hazard of winter weather. In the spring, as the weather begins to warm and the perennials send up new shoots, gradually remove the winter blanket and let the new spring garden emerge.

Summer

Summer is the time to show off your beautiful easy flower garden. When your neighbors' bulbs and spring-flowering perennials have all turned green, your annuals, summer bulbs, and late-flowering perennials will fill your yard with color. As you'll see from these gorgeous combinations, it's easy! Summer is also a great time to sit back and enjoy the birds and butterflies that will flock to your garden—they're so colorful, it's like getting twice as many flowers!

This beautiful easy border mixes annuals, perennials, and bulbs for a riot of summer color. Purple coneflowers, daylilies, and the spikes of glads light up the back of the planting, while a row of mixed annuals repeats the colors in front. An edging of sweet alyssum billows over the walkway.

Annuals like these marigolds, geraniums, and petunias make it easy to fill up a garden with brilliant color all summer long. Not only are they easy to grow, it's fun to try a completely new color scheme each year.

Purple and pink China asters (*Callistephus chinensis*) make an attractive combination with the warm yellows and oranges of pot marigolds (*Calendula officinalis*).

If you let them, self-sowing annuals will create a beautiful easy garden for you. Look how the purple larkspur and hot pink catchfly in this photo have made a garden where only a rosebush grew before.

If you want excitement in a garden, contrasting color combinations are a surefire way to get it. This stunning combination spotlights two of easiest perennials you can grow: spikes of lilac-purple hosta flowers and the red-orange blooms of daylilies.

*Y*ou can plant almost *any* colors together if you soften their contrasts by mixing in plants with silver or gray-green foliage, such as the lamb's-ears (*Stachys byzantina*) in the front of this multi-hued garden.

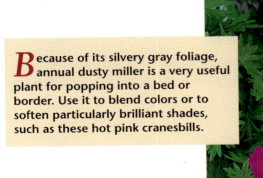

*B*ecause of its silvery gray foliage, annual dusty miller is a very useful plant for popping into a bed or border. Use it to blend colors or to soften particularly brilliant shades, such as these hot pink cranesbills.

*T*his colorful garden combines annuals and perennials to create a burst of summer bloom. Dwarf snapdragons at the front of the border echo the colors of the daylily trumpets behind. They're separated by the showy violet spikes of annual mealycup sage (*Salvia farinacea*).

Planting masses of annuals in bold blocks makes it easy to create an eye-catching garden. This easy-care planting features (*front to back*) white sweet alyssum, watermelon-red petunias and orange pot marigolds, lavender and white ageratum, and brilliant red zinnias.

Perennials make it easy to create a riotous summer display that just gets better every year. This colorful planting features lavender-blue balloon flowers, yellow coreopsis, melon-colored daylilies, hot pink phlox, and, at the far right, purple coneflowers.

*I*n this garden, bearberry clambers over a cluster of rocks, while silvery Japanese painted fern adds a splash of light.

A cluster of pots and tubs and a handful of annuals is all it takes to create a colorful garden on a terrace, deck, patio, or front porch. This grouping features geraniums and petunias, but that's just the beginning of the story. Consider marigolds, moss rose, and even decorative salad crops like red and green leaf lettuce.

Many annuals will provide a spectacular show from seed sown directly in the garden. All you need to do is provide a smooth seedbed and water regularly until the seeds are up and growing vigorously. This meadow garden features pink and white cosmos and orange-and-bronze calliopsis (*Coreopsis tinctoria*).

Clematis is the perfect choice for decorating a lamppost, mailbox, trellis, or any other structure, for that matter. Deciding what color to plant may be the only hard part. Clematis comes in white, red, violet, mauve, blue, yellow, and pale pink.

Morning glories are beautiful easy vines for late summer bloom. Plant gorgeous sapphire blue, white, or rosy purple cultivars to cover a trellis, fence, or wall with flowers.

Get color the first season in your new perennial bed by filling the bed with easy-care annuals each year until the perennials can take over. After that, you can add annuals to accent the perennials.

*F*or a ready-made garden, try planting a couple of flats of annuals. Not only are they inexpensive and easy to grow, but you can try a new color combination every year. This hot-color planting features hot pink petunias, orange marigolds, and dark red celosia plumes.

You don't need to plant a hundred different plants to create a smashing perennial garden—plant masses of a few flowers instead. This showy design features white Shasta daisies, pink and yellow yarrows, red bee balm, and tall yellow perennial sunflowers.

Butterflies are among the most delightful visitors that will come to your garden—I call them "flying flowers." This swallowtail is enjoying the blooms of purple coneflowers (*Echinacea purpurea*).

Sometimes a simple color scheme is the most striking, like the red and white impatiens in front of the red salvia in this garden.

You can't beat daylilies for dependable color that just gets better every year. There are literally thousands of cultivars to choose from. They come in a wide range of colors, from the familiar orange to lemon yellow, rich burgundy, lavender, and nearly white.

Double hollyhocks add a cottage-garden feel to a flower bed. Once established, biennials like hollyhocks often behave like perennials because they self-sow. Be sure to leave some of the spent flowerstalks in the garden to provide flowers for future years.

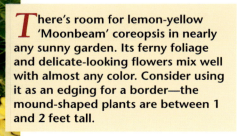

There's room for lemon-yellow 'Moonbeam' coreopsis in nearly any sunny garden. Its ferny foliage and delicate-looking flowers mix well with almost any color. Consider using it as an edging for a border—the mound-shaped plants are between 1 and 2 feet tall.

*L*avatera (*Lavatera trimestris*) is striking and easy-to-grow—a perfect annual for a sunny site. It bears saucer-shaped pink, rose, or white flowers from mid-summer to frost. Here, it's growing with lavender-flowered wild bee balm and yellow daisies.

Birds add movement and color to a flower garden. They are also hardworking garden helpers who will consume countless pesky insects, so it pays to help them feel at home. You can provide housing and a birdbath, and they will enjoy seedheads of flowers like these gloriosa daisies.

For late-season color in your perennial bed, interplant mound-forming dwarf asters with pale yellow 'Moonbeam' coreopsis. Ornamental grasses, tall-growing New England asters, goldenrods, and chrysanthemums are other spectacular plants for a late-summer to fall garden.

For best results, grow zinnias from seed sown where you want the plants to bloom. Transplanting can cause double-flowered types to revert to singles.

Nasturtiums are a snap to grow from seed, thrive in poor soil, and produce loads of colorful, spicy-tasting flowers all summer long.

*I*ndulge yourself with some of the colorful daylily cultivars breeders have developed. Plant them in masses for an easy garden along a driveway, or mix them into a perennial bed with summer-blooming flowers like these perennial sunflowers.

The delicate, butterfly-like blooms of cosmos belie its tough nature. It thrives in warm weather and full sun. Grow it from seeds scattered where you want the plants to bloom.

To add pizzazz to a late-summer garden, pop in some pots of garden chrysanthemums in yellow, burgundy, rust, white, and orange. Butterflies are an extra bonus!

Even the most familiar flowers can add excitement to your garden when you plant new and unusual cultivars, like this stunning fringed red hollyhock.

No sunny garden should be without 'Autumn Joy' sedum. Its broccoli-like flower heads color up in late summer to fall, turning from green to pink to burgundy and finally to rust.

'Goldsturm' rudbeckia is another classic perennial for late-summer-to-fall color. It looks especially good combined with ornamental grasses. Leave the seedheads of both standing for winter interest.

Monarch butterflies visit a variety of flowers, including asters, for nectar during the summer and as they migrate southward in fall. Look for them in your garden!

Wow! For knock-your-socks-off color, try a beautiful easy annual combination like this. Yellow and orange marigolds glow like coals around the blood-red Joseph's coat (*Amaranthus tricolor*), which looks like a flame rising over the ash-silver foliage of dusty miller.

The new smaller sunflowers are show-offs in any sunny garden. They come in a variety of colors—including nearly white, sunny yellow, rust, and orange—and are just as easy to grow as their giant cousins.

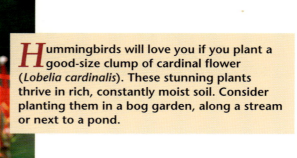

Hummingbirds will love you if you plant a good-size clump of cardinal flower (*Lobelia cardinalis*). These stunning plants thrive in rich, constantly moist soil. Consider planting them in a bog garden, along a stream or next to a pond.

For a garden that will bring you special pleasure, plant flowers along a walkway that you use daily. A few clumps of colorful annuals like the low-growing purple lobelia, red impatiens, single-flowered marigolds, and deep purple verbena growing here are all it takes to bring a smile to your face.

*I*f you try growing a few new flowers every year, you'll keep discovering new favorites. This showy annual is a sunflower called 'Teddy Bear', which bears 6-inch blooms on 2-foot plants. It's hard to miss planted in a group.

*I*t's hard to design a summer-to-fall garden without the spectacular daisy family. From perennial sunflowers and asters to chrysanthemums, golden-rods, sneezeweeds, and heliopsis, they are reliable, easy-care perennials that provide a wealth of bloom.

An El Diablo Drought-Tolerant Garden

Hot-Color Flowers for a Sunny Site

IN THIS DAY AND AGE of water shortages and droughts, gardeners everywhere are cutting down on watering. Sure, mulch helps keep water in the soil, but to really save water, you need to grow plants that thrive in dry soil.

This garden features flowers in vibrant reds and brilliant yellows. All thrive in the hot summer sun, making the El Diablo garden just the ticket for a sunny site that you won't have to water regularly. Although inspired by the blazing colors (and heat!) of the Southwest, this garden can be grown in almost every region of the United States and Canada.

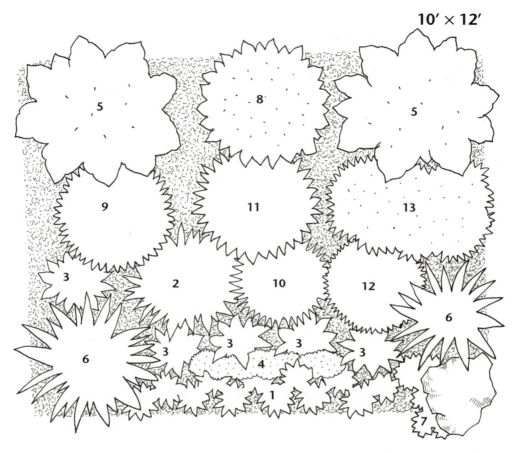

10′ × 12′

1. Blanket flowers
2. Butterfly weed
3. Chili peppers
4. Cilantro
5. Common sunflowers
6. Daylilies
7. Hens-and-chickens

8. Mexican sunflowers
9. Orange coneflower
10. Red-hot poker
11. Sunflower heliopsis
12. Yarrow
13. Yellow cosmos

The hot colors in this garden are positively infernal, but the way it stands up to hot and dry weather is nothing short of heavenly.

PLANTS TO BUY

Buy one of each of the following perennials, unless otherwise noted:

- Butterfly weed
- Daylilies. Buy two.
- Hens-and-chickens. Buy three or four.
- Orange coneflower
- Red-hot poker
- Sunflower heliopsis
- Yarrow

SEEDS TO BUY

Buy one packet of each of the following plants:

- Blanket flowers
- Chili peppers
- Cilantro
- Common sunflowers
- Mexican sunflowers
- Yellow cosmos

THE PLANT GUIDE

PLANTS FOR A DROUGHT-TOLERANT GARDEN

VIVID COLORS abound in this garden. Flowers include striking red cosmos, orange butterfly weed, two types of sunflowers, bright yellow blanket flowers, canary yellow yarrow, and red-hot poker plant. A mat of succulent, cactuslike hens-and-chickens clustered around a rock will add to the painted desert illusion. And how could a Southwestern-style garden be complete without hot chili peppers and tangy cilantro?

Seeds

Buy one packet of each of the following plants. All are annuals, except for the blanket flower.

Blanket flower (*Gaillardia* × *grandiflora*). Some perennials are easy as pie to grow from seed, and blanket flower is one of them. These small, mounded, 12- to 14-inch

plants have bright yellow flowers trimmed in scarlet. If you don't want to grow them from seed, plants are easy to find at garden centers. You'll need to buy a dozen plants. If you can't find blanket flowers or would rather grow an annual in its place, marigolds make a very good substitute. Zones 4 to 9.

Chili peppers (*Capsicum* spp.). There are thousands of peppers to choose from, but I suggest you plant one of the smaller-fruited, more colorful types, including 'Habanero', 'Thai Dragon', or 'Serrano'. Remember, these peppers are green or red and are El Diablo hot! The plants grow to about 2 feet tall. There are also some beautiful heirloom peppers from the Southwest you might try. (See "Where to Buy" on page 226.)

Cilantro (*Coriandrum sativum*). The foliage of this feathery plant, which looks a little bit like flat-leaved parsley, is used for making salsa. It grows about 2 feet tall and bears flat heads of white flowers that look like Queen-Anne's-lace. The flowers eventually yield beige seeds, which are the spice coriander. Cilantro attracts beneficial insects and butterflies.

Mexican sunflower (*Tithonia rotundifolia*). Butterflies love these gorgeous, daisylike, bright orange to scarlet flowers that appear on rangy 4- to 5-foot plants. 'Sundance' and 'Torch' are good cultivars; 'Goldfinger' is an attractive compact type that ranges from 3 to 3½ feet.

Sunflower (*Helianthus annuus*). This is the common sunflower grown for its huge head filled with succulent seeds. You can go for one of the huge cultivars developed for seed production, but I suggest you look at some of the new, smaller (4- to 5-foot) ones developed as garden and cutting flowers. Ornamental types include 'Italian White', 'Sunspot', and 'Velvet Tapestry'.

Yellow cosmos (*Cosmos sulphureus*). Instead of common garden cosmos (*C. bipinnatus*), which has white or pink flowers, look for a red-flowered cultivar of yellow cosmos. It bears daisylike flowers in gold, golden orange, and orange-scarlet. Look for dwarf selections that mature at about 2 or 2½ feet. The Klondyke series cultivars are especially attractive. Try 'Bright Lights' or 'Sunny Red'.

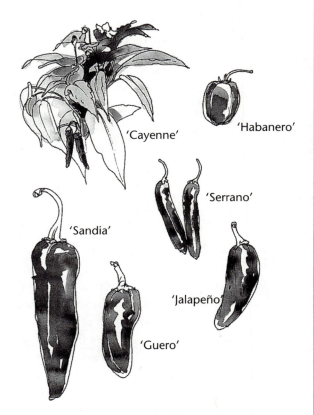

'Cayenne'   'Habanero'   'Serrano'   'Sandia'   'Jalapeño'   'Guero'

These colorful, small-fruited peppers add pizzazz to your El Diablo garden. You can eat them, too.

Plants

You can order perennials through one of the mail-order catalogs listed on page 226, or look for them at your local garden center. Either way, buy one plant of each of the following perennials:

Butterfly weed (*Asclepias tuberosa*). A colorful relative of

WATERWISE OPTIONS

If you really get into drought-tolerant plants and gardens, there's one catalog you shouldn't do without. Plants of the Southwest (Agua Fria, Route 6, Box 11A, Santa Fe, NM 87501) offers plants and seeds for a wide variety of drought-tolerant flowers, herbs, trees, and shrubs. They also have a selection of vegetable cultivars that were developed by the native southwestern tribes, including traditional peppers. This catalog makes for great winter dreaming.

common milkweed, butterfly weed is a deep-rooted native wildflower found in fields throughout much of the eastern half of the country. It produces bright orange flowers all summer long and grows 1 to 3 feet tall. As its name suggests, it is very attractive to butterflies. Zones 3 to 9.

Daylilies (*Hemerocallis* spp. and hybrids). There are thousands of daylilies to choose from, but for this garden, I suggest you buy two with the reddest flowers you can find. You'll get the best quality if you buy field-grown plants, dug up for you on site from a grower in your area. Or try a local nursery. One plant will produce a clump 2 to 3 feet high and wide in a couple of years with an endless parade of flowers for weeks in the summer. Zones 3 to 9.

Hens-and-chickens (*Sempervivum* spp.). Once you start to look, you'll find that there are many colorful cultivars of these endearing but tough, fleshy-leaved, ground-hugging plants, which are sometimes called houseleeks. They generally grow 1 to 3 inches tall and produce white to pink blooms in the summer. Buy three or four plants—perhaps all different—and cluster them around a couple of rocks on the front edge of the bed. Zones 5 to 9.

Orange coneflower (*Rudbeckia fulgida*). The golden orange petals and chocolate brown centers of these easy-to-grow summer daisies light up the El Diablo garden for nearly a month in mid- to late summer. Orange coneflowers are 2 to 3 feet tall and will spread. 'Goldsturm' is an outstanding cultivar. Zones 3 to 9.

Red-hot poker (*Kniphofia uvaria*). Also called torch lily, this clump-forming perennial has grassy-looking leaves. In midsummer, it bears spikes of small, densely packed flowers on 3-foot stems. The flowers at the top of the spikes are bright orange and those lower down are yellow, making them glow like a red-hot poker. Zones 5 to 9.

Sunflower heliopsis (*Heliopsis helianthoides*). This shrubby perennial bears golden daisies with yellow centers in June and July. The plant, which is bushy and somewhat wild-looking, grows 3 to 5 feet tall. Zones 3 to 9.

Yarrows (*Achillea* spp.). Cultivars of yarrow with golden yellow flowers, such as 'Coronation Gold' or 'Gold Plate', look best in this red-and-yellow garden. One plant will spread and reach a height of 3 to 4 feet and will bloom in late spring and summer. Zones 4 to 8.

THE SEASONAL GUIDE

SEASON ONE (JANUARY AND FEBRUARY)

Select a Site

This rectangular garden measures approximately 10 × 12 feet and is filled with a mix of annuals and perennials. You can stick to the garden design on page 220, or reorganize the plants to make the garden fit into your own particular space. Just be sure to put the ornamental sunflowers and the Mexican sunflowers in the back and give the orange coneflowers, sunflower heliopsis, and yarrow plenty of room to spread out.

Buy Seeds, Plants, and Supplies

You don't need a catalog that specializes in exotic, hard-to-find plants to buy what you need for this garden. Most of the annuals and perennials are available in any catalog or from your local garden center or nursery. See "Where to Buy" on page 226 for several of my favorite mail-order sources.

In addition to the seeds and plants listed for this garden, you'll need the following supplies:

• Three 40-pound bags of compost or composted manure. Or substitute homemade compost—one full bin or three wheelbarrows full.

• One 5-pound bag of natural organic fertilizer

• One 50-foot soaker hose, ¾ inch in diameter

• Four large bags of shredded organic mulch, such as pine bark, cedar bark, or pine needles. Or substitute an equivalent amount of your own compost or a mix of compost and shredded leaves.

Start Seeds Indoors

Starting seeds indoors is really very simple. For this garden, you are going to start the chili peppers and the blanket flowers indoors. If you would rather buy the plants, and your local nursery offers hot chili peppers, by all means do so. In that case, you won't need to buy plants until you're ready to plant the garden in Season 2. You'll sow the other annuals—cilantro, cosmos, Mexican sunflowers, and common sunflowers—in Season 2 as well. None of these plants transplant well, but they're all easy to grow from seed sown outdoors where the plants will grow.

There is only room in this garden for four or five chili pepper plants. But since nearly every gardener likes them, I suggest you plant a dozen and give away the extra transplants. To plant them, fill twelve 3-inch peat pots with commercial seed-starting mix. Fill the pots to within 1 inch of the rim.

Water the soil until it is damp but not soggy. (You can do this the night before you sow.) Sprinkle two to three seeds on top of the soil in each pot, and cover with a scant ¹/₁₆ inch of seed-starting mix. Press down lightly.

Place the peat pots in a shallow tray, loosely cover them with clear plastic wrap, and place them in a sunny window in a room with a temperature of 65° to 70°F. If you'd like to get a little more professional, there are several simple plastic seed-starting

---

WHERE TO BUY

You can purchase any of the plants or seeds for the El Diablo garden from the following sources:

• Park Seed Co., Cokesbury Road, Greenwood, SC 29647

• W. Atlee Burpee and Co., 300 Park Avenue, Warminster, PA 18974

If you want to get creative about the peppers and sunflowers you grow, write for catalogs from one of the following companies. All feature a wide variety of unusual types. Plus you'll find a few free recipes!

• Seeds of Change, P.O. Box 15700, Santa Fe, NM 87506

• Shepherd's Garden Seeds, 30 Irene Street, Torrington, CT 06790

greenhouses you can buy that also do an excellent job. You'll find them at your local garden center or featured in some mail-order seed catalogs.

Spray the pots with water from a spray bottle every day to keep the soil evenly moist. In a week or so, the seeds will germinate. Remove the plastic wrap and keep the plants at about 65° to 70°F.

Move your seedlings to a sunny window. When they have their second set of leaves, snip off all but the strongest seedling in each pot with scissors. Continue to care for that one seedling until you are ready to place it outside. Keep your seedlings in as sunny a spot as you can—they should receive at least five hours of sun a day.

Follow the same procedure with the blanket flower seeds, but you will probably want to plant 15 or more peat pots. You'll need between 10 and 12 plants for the garden, but once again, you can always give away any extras.

SEASON TWO (MARCH, APRIL, AND MAY)

Prepare the Site

Depending on where you live, you may need to wait until March or April to actually dig up the soil and prepare your garden site. See "Getting Your Garden Ready to Plant" on page 42 for complete information on preparing the soil. Of course, if you prepared the site the previous fall, you are that much ahead of the game.

To prepare your site, clear away debris and scrape off any grass growing there if you can. You can dig the grass into the soil, but it may come back to haunt you. You are better off removing it completely by slicing it away—roots and all—with a sharp spade. Use it to patch bare spots on your lawn, or turn it upside down on your compost pile.

Spread the compost or other organic matter and the fertilizer on your garden site. Dig the soil to a depth of 6 to 8 inches, using a rotary tiller or a garden fork. Be sure to break up as many clumps as possible. Then rake the area smooth, and you are ready to plant.

Plant the Garden

All of the plants in this garden prefer to grow in the warm soil of late spring or early summer. There's no sense putting these plants or seeds in the ground until all danger of frost is past in your area and nighttime temperatures are consistently above 50°F. They'll just sit shivering in your garden and won't start growing until the temperatures warm up anyway.

Two to three weeks before you are ready to plant, start bringing your pepper and blanket flower plants outdoors to a protected, partially shaded site to allow them to become acclimated to the great outdoors. Start by bringing them out for an hour or so and gradually increase the time they spend outdoors so they can get used to outdoor conditions. Leave them out overnight during the last few days before planting time.

If you have a choice, plant your garden on an overcast, windless day to minimize sunscald and transplant shock. If that's not possible, plant late in the day when the sun is going down and the plants can recover during the cool of the night.

The basic design of this garden calls for the tall plants, such as the sunflowers, to be in the back, the medium-tall plants in the middle, and the short plants in the front. If a circular garden would be better for your site, put the taller plants in the center and surround them with the medium plants, then put the short plants around the edge of the circle. (See the illustration on the opposite page.)

To plant, mark off three equally spaced ovals about 3 feet wide and 5 feet long across the back of the garden. Sow seed for the Mexican sunflowers in the middle oval and the common sunflowers in the ovals on either side. To sow, simply scatter the seeds evenly over the entire surface of the ovals, poke them into the soil about ½ inch deep, and cover them with soil. Tamp the soil down gently.

Two feet in front of the sunflowers on the right, draw another oval 4 feet long and 2 feet wide. Plant the cosmos seeds by evenly sprinkling them over the oval. Then cover them with ½ inch of soil and tamp it down.

Plant the sunflower heliopsis 2 feet in front of the Mexican sunflowers and plant the orange coneflower 2 feet in front of the sunflowers on the left. You can plant more than one of each of these if you want results in a hurry. But even if you plant one of each, in two seasons these plants will spread and fill in their area.

Place the red-hot poker plant in front of the heliopsis, and place the butterfly weed 3 feet away on one side and the yarrow 3 feet away on the other. Plant one daylily on the front left corner of the garden and the other 3 feet back from the front right corner.

In the front right corner of the garden, arrange rocks and plant the hens-and-chickens among the rocks. Plant the blanket flower along the front of the garden between the clump of

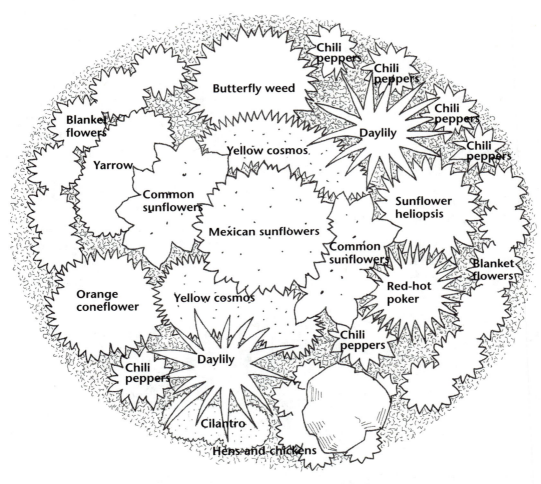

Butterfly weed

Chili peppers

Chili peppers

Chili peppers

Blanket flowers

Yarrow

Yellow cosmos

Daylily

Chili peppers

Common sunflowers

Sunflower heliopsis

Mexican sunflowers

Common sunflowers

Blanket flowers

Orange coneflower

Yellow cosmos

Red-hot poker

Chili peppers

Daylily

Chili peppers

Cilantro

Hens-and-chickens

To create an oval garden you can enjoy from all sides, cluster the tallest sunflowers in the center and fill in around them with shorter plants. Instead of planting regular ovals of sunflowers as you would for the rectangular design, sow the seeds in a more enlongated pattern.

daylilies and the hens-and-chickens.

Draw an oval directly behind the blanket flowers and plant the cilantro there by scattering the seeds evenly over the area. Cover the seeds with ½ inch of soil and tamp it down. Place your pepper plants around and among the central part of the garden wherever it looks as if there's a hole that needs to be filled.

Water everything as you plant it to soak the soil. Continue watering every day to keep the soil moist until the seeds germinate.

SEASON THREE (JUNE, JULY, AND AUGUST)

Minimize Chores and Enjoy Your Garden

Don't mulch your garden until the seedlings emerge from the soil. Once the seedlings are about 3 to 4 inches tall, thin them so the plants are spaced 8 inches apart. When you thin, carefully pinch the plants off by hand or snip them off at ground level with a sharp knife or garden scissors. Pull up the occasional weed by hand.

Install the soaker hose in the garden by snaking it around the plants to cover most of the area. Be sure to leave the connecting end visible so you will be able to attach your conventional garden hose to it easily when you need to water. Since this garden is designed to need little water,

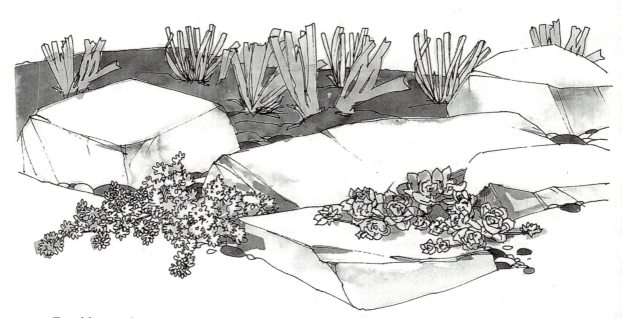

To add an authentic dryland touch to the front of your garden, arrange three or four rocks, as shown here. Then partially cover them with soil and cluster hens-and-chickens around them in a natural-looking arrangement. Plant the hens-and-chickens among the rocks.

you may not have to use a soaker hose at all. But it is good to have it installed just in case you do need it.

Cover the garden—hose and all—with a 2- to 4-inch layer of natural organic mulch, such as compost, shredded bark chips, shredded leaves, or a combination of mulching materials. Don't pile mulch up around the stems of the plants because it can encourage rot. Keep it 1 inch or so away from the smaller plants and 4 inches away from the stems of the shrubbier sunflowers.

It is very important for the perennials in your garden to get adequate water while they are becoming established. If your yard gets $\frac{1}{2}$ inch of rain during the week, you probably won't need to water; otherwise, water weekly. To water, simply attach your garden hose to the soaker hose that snakes though the garden and turn on the water about a quarter turn. Let the water run for one hour. This should keep the soil moist but also give the garden a chance to dry out between watering.

Most of the work is now done. You can relax and enjoy your garden. Remember to pick off any dead or spent blossoms to encourage the plants to continue flowering. Once they bloom, these plants will continue all summer long. Be sure to pick fresh

bouquets for your house and to give to friends.

The peppers and cilantro are primary ingredients for making salsa. Simply grind some up with onions and chopped tomatoes, and you've got a fiery salsa dip for your favorite chips or vegetables.

SEASON FOUR (SEPTEMBER AND OCTOBER)

Prepare Your Garden for Winter

One of the great things about this garden is that it blooms like crazy until late in the fall. But autumn can be dry in many areas, so be sure to water weekly if dry weather does set in. The perennials can suffer the first year and even the second if they don't receive enough rainfall.

If you chose sunflowers that produce seeds, you can harvest them for winter eating. Wait until the seeds are fully developed in the seedheads, then cut them off, and store them in your garage for a few weeks until the seeds fully dry out. If you do nothing, the local birds will come and do the harvesting for you.

Once a frost hits your area and kills the pepper plants, cilantro, cosmos, and sunflowers, pull them up, break them into smaller pieces, and toss them in the compost bin.

Once the really cold weather sets in and your perennials are looking pretty ragged, cut them off 1 or 2 inches above the soil line. Remove the soaker hose, drain it, and store it for the winter.

When the ground is fully frozen, cover your garden with a layer of shredded leaves or the boughs from a Christmas tree to provide a thermal blanket to protect the plants from cold, dry winter winds and the heaving of the soil as it freezes and thaws.

Take notes about how your garden performed this year. You may want to make a few changes, such as adding a few plants like culinary sage, artemisia, or grasses that can give the garden a slightly different look.

Chances are, you won't need to dig and divide your thriving perennials until next year—even later in the case of the daylilies. Fall is the very best time to dig up, separate, and replant perennials.

When that time comes, dig up the entire plant and gently pull the root ball apart so you are left with two or three smaller plants rather than one big one. You must dig up and separate most of the perennials in this garden every three or four years when the center dies or the plant loses vigor and declines. But don't disturb the butterfly weed: It has a very deep taproot and doesn't tolerate disturbances well.

Up Against a Wall

A Border to Dress Up a Wall or Fence

IF YOUR NEIGHBORHOOD IS TYPICAL, *every house on your block has clipped junipers and yews planted like pillows against the foundation. This garden gives you a chance to do something a little more fun with your home's foundation.*

Planting a flower border eliminates the endless pruning that typical foundation plantings require. And this garden also gives you loads of flowers to enjoy, whether you're looking out from inside your house, driving up to your house after a long day at work, or taking them indoors in bouquets. All it asks in return is a spot on the sunny side of your house. This garden would look just as pretty against a fence, garage, or shed.

8' × 20'

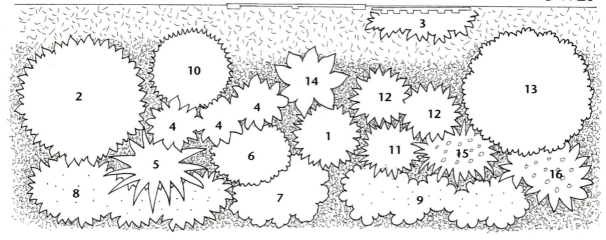

1. Balloon flower
2. Bigleaf hydrangea
3. Clematis
4. Dahlias
5. Daylily
6. Garden mum
7. Lady's-mantle
8. Narrow-leaf zinnias
9. Nasturtiums
10. New England aster
11. Peach-leaved bellflower
12. Phlox
13. Shrub rose
14. Yellow foxglove
15. Daffodils
16. Tulips

SEEDS TO BUY

Buy one packet of each of the following annuals:

- Narrow-leaf zinnias
- Nasturtiums

BULBS TO BUY

Buy a dozen bulbs of each of the following:

- Daffodils
- Tulips

Add excitement to your foundation planting with these colorful easy-care flowers.

PLANTS TO BUY

Unless otherwise noted, buy one plant of each of the following perennials:

- Balloon flower
- Bigleaf hydrangea
- Clematis
- Dahlias. Buy two or three.
- Daylily
- Garden mum
- Lady's-mantle
- New England aster
- Peach-leaved bellflower
- Phlox. Buy two.
- Shrub rose
- Yellow foxglove

THE PLANT GUIDE

PLANTS FOR A TALL BORDER

THIS GARDEN features tall, spiky flowers that will look great against your house, along with shorter plants that will create attractive layers of bloom. It features a combination of easy-care shrubs, a climbing vine, bulbs, perennials, and annuals that will give you colorful blooms from early spring until frost.

In early spring, tulips and daffodils start off the show. They are followed by the rose and clematis in early summer. During the warm summer months, flowers from balloon flowers, daylilies, lady's-mantle, nasturtiums, phlox, peach-leaved bellflowers, yellow foxgloves, zinnias, and a hydrangea provide nonstop bloom. Later in the summer and into the fall, asters, dahlias, and garden mums continue the show. Your foundation never dreamed it could look this good!

Seeds

You'll grow the zinnias and nasturtiums for this garden from seed. Buy one packet of each.

Narrow-leaf zinnias (*Zinnia angustifolia*). Another heat-tolerant annual, narrow-leaf zinnias have daisy-like flowers with dark purplish black button centers. The species has orange petals marked with yellow stripes. Although there are also pink-, yellow-, and white-flowered cultivars, stick to orange ones for this garden. Plants are covered with flowers all summer and are about 8 inches tall.

Nasturtiums (*Tropaeolum majus*). These colorful annuals tolerate drought and poor soil, and they bear eye-catching red, orange, and yellow blooms all summer. The leaves and flowers are peppery-tasting—they're great added to salads. For this garden, be sure to pick a compact type. (There are vining ones that will climb to 6 feet.) 'Whirlybird' or variegated-leaved 'Alaska' are both good choices. Both grow to between 8 and 12 inches tall.

Plants

Buy one plant of each of the following perennials, unless otherwise noted. Dahlias are tender perennials grown from tuberous roots; you can buy either dahlia roots or potted plants.

Balloon flower (*Platycodon grandiflorus*). This plant is named for its balloon-shaped buds that swell up until they burst open into 2- to 3-inch blue, white, or pink starry flowers. Plants are 1 to 3 feet tall and bear spikes of flowers for weeks during the summer. Zones 3 to 8.

Dahlias (*Dahlia* spp.). Dahlias come in a wide range of flower colors, sizes, and types. Flowers can be any color but true blue and range from 2 to 12 inches across. They may resemble daisies, chrysanthemums, or waterlilies and will bloom from summer to frost. For this garden, buy two or three dahlias that will reach 2 to 3 feet tall in any color or blossom shape you prefer. Although you can grow dahlias from seed, you'll get faster results if you buy roots or plants. Your local garden center may have potted plants for sale, or you can order from one of the companies

listed in "Where to Buy" on page 242. At the end of the season, you can dig up your plants, store the tuberous roots over winter, and replant them the following spring.

Daylilies (*Hemerocallis* spp. and hybrids). These indestructible perennials will produce a clump that is 2 to 3 feet across in a couple of years and produce an endless parade of flowers all summer long. Flowers come in yellows, oranges, maroons, and nearly white. Buy any color you like. Zones 2 to 9.

Garden mum (*Chrysanthemum × morifolium*, also sold as *Dendranthema × grandiflorum*). Even nongardeners recognize the garden mum as a traditional sign of fall. Flower colors range from white through pink, rose, red, burgundy, gold, yellow, and cream, and the plants vary in size from $1\frac{1}{2}$ to 5 feet tall. Buy any color that appeals to you. Be sure to buy a hardy garden mum, though, and not one of the potted florist mums sold for indoor gift plants. Florist mums will survive from year to year but generally won't manage to flower in the garden before frost destroys the blooms. Zones 4 to 9.

Lady's-mantle (*Alchemilla mollis*). This mound-shaped plant has attractive round and pleated leaves and frothy spikes of yellow-green flowers that bloom in spring and early summer. Plants are about 1 foot tall and are attractive used as edging plants along a pathway. Zones 3 to 8.

New England aster (*Aster novae-angliae*). This hardy perennial aster is a native American wildflower that blooms from summer into fall. Gardeners have many improved cultivars to choose from in heights ranging from 3 to 6 feet and in colors ranging from white and pale pink to deep pink and purple-blue. 'Alma Potschke' has dark pink flowers, 'Hella Lacy', royal purple, and 'Treasure', lavender-blue. Plants will spread. Zones 3 to 8.

Peach-leaved bellflower (*Campanula persicifolia*). Bell-shaped blue or white flowers adorn this classic perennial in the summer. Plants form attractive clumps and grow 1 to 3 feet tall, depending on the cultivar you select. Zones 3 to 7.

Phlox (*Phlox paniculata*). Garden phlox is a classic, summer-blooming perennial that's a must for this garden. Plants bear domed clusters of white, pink, or magenta flowers on 2- to 3-foot plants. Look for mildew-resistant cultivars, such as 'David', 'Franz Schubert', 'Eva Cullum', and 'Omega'. Buy two plants. Zones 3 or 4 to 8.

Yellow foxglove (*Digitalis grandiflora*, also sold as *D. ambigua*). Unlike common foxglove, which is a biennial, yellow foxglove is a long-lived perennial. It blooms in summer and bears spikes of pale yellow bell-shaped flowers on 2- to 3-foot plants. Zones 3 to 8.

Bulbs

Buy a dozen each of these classic bulbs to brighten your garden in spring:

Daffodils (*Narcissus* spp.). When you're considering daffodils, don't think you're limited to good old 'King Alfred'. There are hundreds—even thousands—of daffodils to choose from. Look at your local garden center or in mail-order catalogs and pick your favorites. When you buy, spend a little more to get the larger, better-quality bulbs rather than the super-cheap assortments. For more on buying quality bulbs, see the illustration on page 167. Buy a dozen bulbs. Zones 4 to 9, depending on the species and cultivar you select.

Tulips (*Tulipa* spp.). You'll find tulips displayed right next to the daffodils in your local garden center or listed near them in your favorite catalog. Buy a dozen bulbs of any color or colors you like. Unlike daffodils, tulips generally don't multiply from year to year. In fact, they tend to peter out and need replacing every few years. Darwin hybrid tulips, single late tulips, and many species tulips are generally long-lived and dependable. Zones 5 to 8.

Shrubs and Vines

Buy one of each of the following shrubs and vine:

Bigleaf hydrangea (*Hydrangea macrophylla*). My favorite bigleaf hy-drangea is 'Nikko Blue', which will become 4 to 5 feet tall and equally wide in three or four years. It will be covered with globe-shaped flowers most of the summer. If your soil is acid, they'll be blue. If the soil is neutral, you'll have some pink and some blue flowers. Zones 6 to 9.

Clematis (*Clematis* spp.). Clematis adds height and color to

Jackman clematis

'Nelly Moser' clematis

'Crimson Star' clematis

Choosing a clematis is like eating potato chips—bet you can't choose just one. There are so many beautiful cultivars to choose from that you may end up with a couple of trellises to display your favorites.

this border as it clambers up a trellis attached to the fence or wall behind it. There are dozens of clematis to choose from, and contrary to popular opinion, they are actually very hardy and easy to grow. 'Jackmanii' is a classic purple-blue, 'Nelly Moser' has mauve-pink blooms, and 'Crimson Star' has red flowers. All of these are vigorous, heavy-blooming plants that will cover trellises and climbing roses with color later in the season when roses are blooming only sporadically. The vines can grow 15 feet long. Zones 3 or 4 to 8,

depending on the cultivar you select.

Shrub roses (*Rosa* spp.). For this garden, look for one of the wonderful new shrub roses that are trouble-free and everblooming. Look for pink-flowered 'Royal Bonica', red-flowered 'F. J. Grootendorst', or one of the very beautiful David Austin English roses, such as 'Graham Thomas', 'Mary Rose', or 'Heritage'. Shrub roses will range from 4 to 5 feet tall or more and spread as wide, depending on the cultivar you select. Most are hardy in Zones 4 or 5 to 10.

THE SEASONAL GUIDE

SEASON ONE (JANUARY AND FEBRUARY)

Select a Site

This garden is approximately 6 to 8 feet wide and 20 feet long. It has been designed to be planted along a house,

garage, or fence. Notice that the garden design on page 234 stands away from the wall about 1½ to 2 feet. This leaves enough room so that you can reach the plants in the back without stepping on the soil. Keep this path mulched so it doesn't get filled with weeds.

As you consider sites, keep in mind that this garden needs a site in full sun. That means it needs at least six full hours of sunshine each day for the plants to thrive and produce their best flowers. A south-facing site would provide the most sun, so it would be ideal. A site that faces east would be my second choice for this garden, and a west-facing one would be third. The flowers in this garden won't receive enough sun to bloom in a north-facing site.

This garden definitely needs a solid backdrop to be its most beautiful. Furthermore, you are going to install a trellis for the clematis, so a wall of some kind is very important for attaching it.

Buy Seeds, Plants, Bulbs, and Supplies

You probably can buy most of the seeds and plants for this garden at local garden centers and nurseries once they have their spring displays ready. But it's fun to order by mail, too. For a list of mail-order companies that sell perennials, see "Where to Buy" on page 242.

Most of the seeds and plants in this garden can be planted in late spring or early summer, but as you get ready for planting, keep in mind that you'll be planting the daffodils and tulips in the fall.

In addition to the seeds, plants, and bulbs listed for this garden, you'll need the following supplies:

• Four 40-pound bags of compost or composted manure. Or substitute homemade compost—one full bin or three wheelbarrows full.

• Two 4-cubic-foot bags of additional organic matter, such as compost, chopped leaves, or rotted sawdust

• One 5-pound bag of natural organic fertilizer

PICK A SITE YOU'LL ENJOY

In most parts of the country, you can't do much to prepare a garden site in the middle of winter. But while you're cooped up indoors, you can dream about where you would enjoy the sight of your perennials the most. Then once spring arrives, you'll be ready to dig in. For example, if you locate this garden near a window, you'll also be able to enjoy your flowers from indoors. Or maybe the best site is against a fence across from the kitchen window. Once you've picked a site *you* like, make sure it suits your plants, too.

WHERE TO BUY

It's probably easiest to buy the zinnia and nasturtium seeds at your local garden center or hardware store.

You can order the perennials and shrubs from any of the following sources:

• W. Atlee Burpee & Co., 300 Park Avenue, Warminster, PA 18974

• Wayside Gardens, 1 Garden Lane, Hodges, SC 29695-0001

• White Flower Farm, P.O. Box 50, Litchfield, CT 06759-0050

White Flower Farm offers a good selection of dahlias, but you can also order them from the following companies:

• Dutch Gardens, P.O. Box 200, Adelphia, NJ 07710

• Park Seed Company, Cokesbury Road, Greenwood, SC 29647

All of the companies listed above sell hardy bulbs by mail as well.

• One 50-foot soaker hose, ¾ inch in diameter

• Six large bags of shredded organic mulch, such as pine bark, cedar bark, or pine needles. Or substitute an equivalent amount of your own compost or a mix of compost and shredded leaves.

• One 6- to 8-foot trellis

SEASON TWO
(MARCH, APRIL, AND MAY)

Prepare the Site

Spring is the best time to start preparing this garden. Before you begin, make sure the soil is no longer frozen and that it is dry enough to work. See "Getting Your Garden Ready to Plant" on page 42 for complete information on preparing the soil. Except for the dahlias, nasturtiums, and zinnias, all of the plants are pretty hardy and should be planted before the really warm days of summer arrive.

Be sure to have a soil test done a few weeks before you're ready to plant. In a foundation garden, checking soil pH is especially important since the soil next to a foundation can be quite alkaline from an accumulation of gypsum frequently used in building foundations. Contact your local Cooperative Extension Service office (listed under city or county governments in your telephone book) for a soil test kit, or buy a do-it-yourself kit at your garden center; they're easy to use. If you need to lower the pH, follow their directions on how much sulphur to use.

When you're ready to prepare your site, first mark off the plot with short stakes so you don't lose track of

A maintenance path makes it easy to reach flowers in the back of your border and lets you weed without crushing front-row blooms. It also makes it easy for you to reach that part of your house for painting, cleaning gutters, washing windows, and other necessary chores.

its dimensions. Then check and double-check to make sure there are no underground power cables running from the house through your site. After you've made sure you won't be disturbing any wires, clear away rocks and debris. Use a sharp spade

to remove any grass that is growing there. Use the grass you've removed to patch spots in your lawn, or place it upside down on your compost pile.

Next, spread the organic matter, natural organic fertilizer, and any sulfur recommended by your soil test results evenly over the entire site. To incorporate all the soil amendments and make the soil as crumbly and smooth as possible, till the soil with a rotary tiller or garden spade to a depth of 8 inches. Rake the area smooth, and you are ready to plant.

Plant the Garden

A cloudy, overcast day is best for planting this garden because it protects the young plants from the hot rays of the sun. If you can't wait for a cloudy day, at least plant everything late in the day to minimize the sun's harsh effect.

When you are ready to plant, bring all of the plants and the trellis outdoors to the garden site. If you're planting in early spring, wait until all danger of frost has passed to plant the dahlias and sow the zinnia and nasturtium seeds. They'll appreciate the warmer soil later in the season.

Start by arranging your plants in the spots where you want to plant them. Then step back and look at the garden before you plant anything to see if you like the arrangement. That way you can adjust the positions of the plants easily. You can follow the garden design on page 234 that I've provided, or rearrange it in any way that suits you. For example, if you have a window near the right side of your site, you may want to move the trellis over a bit and adjust the other plants accordingly.

Install the trellis first by securing it firmly into the ground. If you are following my design, put it on the right side of the garden, about 6 feet from the end. If you like, you can attach the trellis to the house. If you do, keep the bottom end no more than 1 foot off the ground. This gives the trellis additional height and helps to prevent the wood from rotting in the ground.

Next, decide where to plant the hydrangea. Using a stick or trowel, draw a circle approximately 5 feet in diameter in the soil on the far left side of the garden bed and place the hydrangea in the center. Then draw a circle 4 feet in diameter on the right side toward the back and place the rose there. Don't forget to allow for the narrow maintenance path at the back of the garden.

The right edge of the trellis should be about 1 foot away from the left side of the rose circle. Place the clematis at the base of the trellis. Draw an oval that's 1 foot wide and 4 feet long about 3 feet in front of the clematis. Place the two phlox in this oval, spacing them about 15 inches apart. (The extra spacing allows for the maintenance path to go between the clematis and phlox—leave enough space so you don't walk on the clematis roots.)

Now locate the yellow foxglove and aster plants between the phlox and hydrangea, as shown in the garden design on page 234. Plant them about 1 foot in front of your maintenance path. Then position the daylily, dahlias (if you are planting them now; otherwise leave room for them), garden mum, balloon flower, and peach-leaved bellflower, as shown in the design. Plant the lady's mantle in the center of the border in front of the garden mum. If you've followed my design, you'll have room in the front of the garden for the zinnias and nasturtiums and space for the daffodils and tulips in front of the shrub rose.

Starting at the back of the garden, put in each plant in the site you've selected by digging a hole large enough to hold the root ball. (If you have bareroot plants, make sure there is enough room to spread the roots out in the hole.) Make each hole only deep enough so that the crown of the plant—the point where the top of the plant meets the roots—is at ground level. To refill the hole, gather the soil around the plant and press down firmly with your hands. Water thoroughly after planting and then every few days until the plants are established.

Later in the spring, after the ground is thoroughly warm and there is no longer any chance of frost, you can plant the dahlias and sow seeds of the zinnias and nasturtiums. The dahlias need to be planted a bit differently than the rest of the plants. Plant them by digging a hole 6 inches deep and slightly larger than the tuberous roots. Place the roots in the bottom of the trench and cover them with soil. Drive a 3- to 4-foot wooden stake next to the crown of each plant. As the dahlia sprouts, fill in the hole with soil and press down firmly. (See the illustration on this page for how to plant a dahlia tuber.)

To sow the seeds, use your garden rake to smooth out the soil in two long narrow bands across the front of the garden. Sprinkle the zinnia seeds on the spot to the left of the lady's mantle, cover with ¼ inch of fine soil, and press down firmly with your hands.

Nasturtium seeds are rather large. Distribute these seeds evenly across

Dahlias need to be tied to a sturdy stake to show their flowers to best advantage. To avoid damaging the roots, position the stake when you plant. As the dahlia grows, tie the stem to the stake with soft yarn or strips of cloth.

the remainder of the garden border, spacing them about 6 inches apart. Poke the nasturtium seeds into the soil just a little more than ½ inch deep, cover with soil, and firm down with your hand. (Next year, once you've planted the tulips and daffodils, you can fill in between them with nasturtiums to hide the fading bulb foliage.) Keep the soil evenly moist until the seeds germinate in about a week to ten days.

The last step in the planting process is to mulch your garden. But before you do that, snake your soaker hose through the garden in some sort of S-curve, covering as much of the garden as possible. Be sure to leave the connecting end visible so you can find it. Then cover the entire garden and the soaker hose with a 2- to 4-inch-thick layer of natural organic mulch such as shredded bark. Natural organic mulch, as opposed to synthetic landscape fabric or weed mats, is essential for the health and well-being of this garden. Since most of the plants are perennials, you won't till the soil each year to add extra organic matter. Instead, the mulch you put down is going to decompose over the course of the season and add organic matter to the garden for you.

SEASON THREE (JUNE, JULY, AND AUGUST)

Minimize Chores and Enjoy Your Garden

Once the warm weather of summer begins and the rains slow down, you should water your garden on a regular basis. To water, simply attach your conventional garden hose to the soaker hose and turn on the water about a quarter turn. You want to soak the ground to a depth of 6 to 8 inches. Depending on your soil conditions and water flow, this could take anywhere from one to two hours. Don't water again for another week. It's good for your plants if the soil dries out a bit between waterings.

To help promote a more compact growth habit with more flowers, pinch off 1 or 2 inches from the tips of the aster and garden mum plants once a week until mid-July. Don't do it after that or you won't get any flowers in the fall.

The shrub roses I've recommended for this garden shouldn't have any problems with black spot or mildew. They may be attacked by aphids, though. If they are, spray the plants with a hard stream of water from your hose to knock them off. Insecticidal soap works, too, but a few sessions with the hose should be enough. Ladybugs will help with aphid control.

You'll be able to make some beautiful bouquets from this garden—balloon flowers, bellflowers, foxgloves, and roses all look nice together. And hydrangea blossoms are very stunning indeed.

Pinching asters and garden mums encourages the plants to branch and produce more flowers. It also keeps them shorter and more compact. Don't pinch after mid-July, though, or you may pinch off flower buds.

SEASON FOUR (SEPTEMBER AND OCTOBER)

Plant the Hardy Bulbs

You will start seeing catalogs and displays for daffodils and tulips along about August. It's fine to buy them as soon as you like, but resist the temptation to plant them before Labor Day. When you're ready to plant, bring all the bulbs out to the garden, and arrange them in clusters of three to five bulbs on the right side of the garden, just behind the nasturtiums.

Pull up or move any nasturtiums that may have invaded their spot.

Dig the holes with a trowel or a special bulb planter. Plant the daffodils 8 to 10 inches deep and the tulips 6 to 8 inches deep. Place the bulbs in the holes root side down and fill in the holes.

Next spring, after your garden bulbs have bloomed, don't cut their tops off. You can cut off any flower stems, but you must leave the leaves until they turn brown because they are making food and flowers for next season's display. Once the leaves turn brown in midsummer, however, you can cut them off and compost them. Or just leave them where they are, and they'll add organic matter to the soil without any help from you.

Prepare the Garden for Winter

This garden will keep right on blooming until really cold weather arrives. As the cold weather approaches and the frost kills off the plants, pull up the zinnias and nasturtiums and place them in the compost pile. Cut the spent perennials down to within 1 to 2 inches of the ground, composting their tops. Remove the soaker hose, drain it, and store it for the winter.

The asters, dahlias, and garden mums will continue to bloom until almost Thanksgiving. Be sure to pick their flowers for wonderful fall bouquets that are usually very fragrant.

If you would like to save your dahlia plants for next year, here's how. After a hard frost kills the tops of the plants, cut off all the top growth and dig up the dahlias from the ground. Brush the soil off the tuberous roots, and let them dry in a warm, dry place for a few days. Store them over winter in a bed of peat moss, sawdust, or leftover potting soil in a cool (45°F), dry place that is protected from mice. Plant them again next spring.

Once the ground is frozen or as cold as it is going to get, cover the entire bed with a 2- to 4-inch-thick layer of compost, shredded leaves, or a combination of the two. This blanket protects the perennials from harsh winter weather.

You can also prune the clematis back to within 4 to 6 inches of the ground. It will produce all-new growth next year. For best growth and bloom, place 1 tablespoon of lime at the base of the clematis early next spring.

You won't have to prune your hydrangea for at least three or four years

while it gets established. Then just prune it by picking the flowers while it is in bloom or immediately after it blooms.

Winter care for roses is also uncomplicated. The roses I've recommended don't need any special winter protection south of Zone 4 or 5, depending on which rose you've planted. If you like, you can mound up a 3- to 4-inch-thick layer of compost around the crown or base of the rose. Try to remove any leaves that may harbor diseases or insects over the winter.

Pruning roses is very simple. Early in the spring, just as the new pink buds are beginning to emerge, prune off one third of the rose's height at a point just above a pink rosebud. Cut the stem at a 45-degree angle slanting away from the bud for best results. Also, cut out any dead or broken stems.

As soon as the ground has warmed up and the roses are really beginning to grow and set new leaves, sprinkle 1 or 2 tablespoons of Epsom salts at the base of each rosebush and mulch heavily with compost or composted horse manure, if you can get it. Your roses will love it!

A Beautiful Easy Rock Garden

Tough but Tiny Plants for a Sunny Site

ROCK GARDENS ARE AMONG the most satisfying kinds of gardens you can have. Many rock-garden plants form jewel-like mats of color. You can while away dozens of peaceful hours tucking plants in among the rocks and nurturing each individual plant to its fullest potential. Also, each plant really shows up among the rocks!

This garden is a perfect choice if you happen to have a lot of rocks on your property. If you don't, don't despair. You can create an attractive rock garden with a few good-size flat rocks purchased at a local quarry. Or consider a simple raised bed for this garden.

6′ × 14′

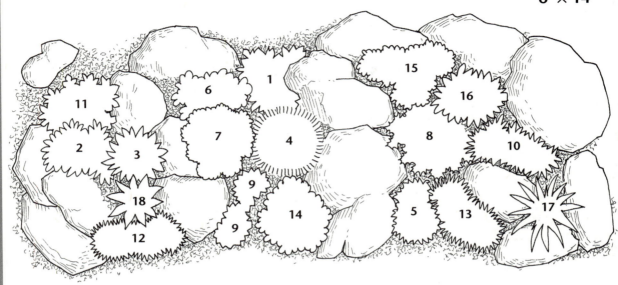

1. Alpine strawberries
2. Basket-of-gold
3. Blanket flower
4. Blue flax
5. Candytuft
6. Carpathian harebell
7. Catmint
8. Cranesbill
9. Hens-and-chickens
10. Lavender
11. Miniature rose
12. Moss phlox
13. Pinks
14. Sedum
15. Thyme
16. Violet sage
17. Daffodils
18. Tulips

BULBS TO BUY

Buy a dozen of each of the following bulbs:

- Daffodils
- Tulips

This garden is so much fun that if you don't already have rocks on your property, you may want to add some.

PLANTS TO BUY

Buy one of each of the following perennials, unless otherwise noted:

- Alpine strawberries
- Basket-of-gold
- Blanket flower
- Blue flax
- Candytuft
- Carpathian harebell
- Catmint
- Cranesbill
- Hens-and-chickens. Buy two.
- Lavender
- Miniature rose
- Moss phlox
- Pinks
- Sedum
- Thyme
- Violet sage

THE PLANT GUIDE

PLANTS FOR A SUNNY ROCK GARDEN

THIS GARDEN will bloom early in the spring with tiny daffodils, tulips, basket-of-gold, and moss phlox. The earliest spring bloomers are followed by candytuft and tiny miniature roses. During the summer, alpine strawberries, bellflowers, blanket flowers, cranesbills, lavender, pinks, sedums, thyme, and violet sage provide color. And every rock garden needs a few hens-and-chickens tucked among the rock crannies.

Plants

Buy one plant of each of the following rock-garden perennials, unless otherwise noted:

Alpine strawberries (*Fragaria vesca*). Plants spread by creeping stolons and make an attractive evergreen mat. They produce pretty white flowers and tasty but tiny red berries off and on during the summer. Zones 5 to 9.

Basket-of-gold (*Aurinia saxatilis*). Also known as goldentuft and rock madwort (believe it or not!), this easy-to-grow perennial covers itself with tiny, four-petaled, bright yellow flowers in April or May. Plants have gray-green leaves and are 10 to 12 inches tall. Zones 3 to 7.

Blanket flower (*Gaillardia × grandiflora*). This is a native American wildflower that's easy to grow from seeds or plants. It forms small, 12- to 14-inch mounds that bear bright, daisylike flowers that are deep orange or brick red with petals tipped in yellow. Flowers appear from June to September. Zones 4 to 9.

Blue flax (*Linum perenne*). This is a relative of commercial flax, which is the source of linseed oil and linen cloth. The plants produce loads of light blue, 1-inch flowers on 20-inch stems covered with needlelike leaves.

Established plants form nice clumps that rarely need division. They bloom in June and July. Zones 4 to 9.

Candytuft (*Iberis sempervirens*). Brilliant white is the only way to describe the flowers of this hardworking perennial groundcover. The 6- to 12-inch plants are covered with flat-topped clusters of tiny honey-scented flowers in spring. The flowers are held above dark green, needlelike foliage that's evergreen. 'Autumn Snow' reblooms in the fall. Zones 3 to 9.

Carpathian harebell (*Campanula carpatica*). A mound-shaped plant that ranges from 8 to 18 inches tall, Carpathian harebell bears hundreds of light blue or white cup-shaped flowers in the spring and summer. 'Blue Clips', often sold as 'Blue Chips', is a popular cultivar. Zones 3 to 8.

Catmint (*Nepeta × faassenii*). A close relative of catnip, catmint produces a cloud of blue-violet flowers atop mound-shaped plants. Plants bloom in late spring and continue until September, especially if you give them a haircut when they get scraggly looking. Plants are 1½ to 2 feet tall; 'Six Hills Giant' reaches 3 feet. Zones 3 to 8.

Cranesbills (*Geranium* spp.). Another name for this popular perennial is hardy geranium, but don't confuse these cold-tolerant perennials with the potted annual geraniums that appear everywhere around Memorial Day; they're actually in the genus *Pelargonium*. Cranesbills are mound-shaped plants that range from 6 inches to 2 feet tall and bear five-petaled flowers and attractive, deeply cut leaves. They bloom in spring and early summer. Two of my favorites are blood red cranesbill (*G. sanguineum*), which has magenta-red flowers, and wood cranesbill (*G. sylvaticum*), which has violet-blue flowers. Zones 3 to 8.

Hens-and-chickens (*Sempervivum* spp.). Hens-and-chickens is a plant you need to look at up close to really appreciate. Once you start to look, you'll find many charming cultivars of these tough, fleshy-leaved, ground-hugging plants, which are sometimes also called houseleeks. Look around and pick your favorite types—all of them are drought-tolerant and couldn't be easier to grow. Rosettes range from all green or green with a spidery white webbing to green and red, green and lavender, and all red or purple. Individual rosettes may be 1 to 4 inches wide, but a clump can spread to 18 inches. There's room for at least two clumps in this garden—and perhaps more! Zones 5 to 9.

Lavender (*Lavandula angustifolia*). Many herbs appreciate the well-drained soil that a rock garden provides, and lavender is no exception. Lavender is a shrubby herb with needlelike gray or blue-green foliage and produces spikes of very fragrant, lavender-purple flowers throughout the summer. Plants reach about 2 feet. 'Hidcote' and 'Munstead' are two popular cultivars you can easily find. Zones 5 to 9.

Moss phlox (*Phlox subulata*). This ground-hugging phlox forms a dense, creeping mat of needlelike leaves, which is covered with magenta, pink, lavender-blue, or white flowers in April and May. It's the one you see carpeting sloping yards with color every spring. Zones 2 to 9.

Pinks (*Dianthus* spp.). Old-fashioned garden pinks make great additions to any rock garden. They have attractive blue-green foliage that's evergreen. And in spring and summer, they produce hundreds of small, fragrant, five-petaled flowers with edges that look like they were cut with pinking shears. Flowers come in pink, rose, and white; many types bear bicolor flowers. Look for maiden pinks (*D. deltoides*), cheddar pinks (*D. gratianopolitanus*), or cottage pinks (*D. plumarius*). Plants range anywhere from 6 inches to 2 feet, depending on the species and cultivar you select. Many pinks will self-sow. Zones 3 to 9.

Moss phlox

Cheddar pinks

Alpine strawberry

Hens-and-chickens

Creeping plants are the glory of any rock garden as they cascade over boulders and fill the spaces between rocks. The plants shown here would be at home in a well-drained sunny site in any garden.

Roses (*Rosa* spp.). For this garden, you'll want a low-growing rose that doesn't get any taller than about 2 feet. You can look at true miniature roses, but one of the best of the smaller roses is a polyanthus type called 'The Fairy'. 'The Fairy' produces clouds of double pale pink flowers all summer long. Zones 5 to 9.

Sedums (*Sedum* spp.). Sedums are drought-tolerant perennials that have fleshy leaves and creep along the ground or form attractive clumps. You'll find dozens of types that are superb for rock gardens—you may want to add several over the years. Kamschatka sedum (*S. kamtschaticum*) produces bright yellow flowers in the summer. Plants are 6 to 9 inches tall. October daphne (*S. sieboldii*) is a low, clump-forming type that bears pink flowers in the fall atop 6- to 9-inch plants. Zones 3 to 8.

Thyme (*Thymus vulgaris*). In addition to being a wonderful herb, common thyme makes an attractive shrubby addition to a rock garden or the front of a perennial border. Plants have tiny, pungent leaves, are evergreen, and reach about 2 feet in height. They have small pale blue or white flowers. Zones 6 to 9.

Violet sage (*Salvia* × *superba*). The best of the violet sages for this garden is 'East Friesland'. It produces 18-inch-tall spikes of deep purple flowers from June until September. If you'd like to grow an herbal rock garden, though, you could easily replace this plant with the common herb sage. Zones 4 to 7.

Bulbs

Buy at least a dozen of each of the following spring-blooming bulbs—more if you like. Instead of the tall, long-stemmed hardy daffodils and tulips you see growing everywhere, look for diminutive species and cultivars that are in scale with this garden. Check out the offerings at your local garden center, or read the descriptions in mail-order bulb catalogs. If you like, you can add other small bulbs to this garden, including glory-of-the-snow (*Chionodoxa luciliae*), grape hyacinths (*Muscari* spp.), snowdrops (*Galanthus* spp.), and squills (*Scilla* spp.).

Daffodils (*Narcissus* spp.). Rather than worry about names of daffodils to buy, just look for bulbs that produce small flowers and stand 6 to 8 inches tall. A couple to look for include cyclamineus narcissus (*N. cyclamineus*)—'February Gold' and 'Jack Snipe' are good choices—as well as angel's-tears (*N. triandrus*) and jonquils (*N. jonquilla*). Zones 4 or 5 to 9, depending on the species and cultivar you select.

Tulips (*Tulipa* spp.). Look for 6- to 8-inch plants described as wild or botanical tulips. (Make sure they weren't wild-collected, though; generally if you buy named cultivars, you're safe.) Kaufmanniana tulips are a good choice: They have leaves striped with brown and close their star-shaped flowers at night. Zones 4 to 8.

THE SEASONAL GUIDE

SEASON ONE (JANUARY AND FEBRUARY)

Select a Site

Spend some time during the winter looking for the perfect site for this garden. Although a rock garden can be any size you like, this one is about 6 feet wide by 14 feet long. The main requirements are full sun—at least six hours per day—and well-drained soil. When you prepare the site for this garden, you'll improve the soil drainage, so just stay away from areas with soggy soil. A gently sloping site in full sun at the edge of the lawn is fine, or the side of your driveway is ideal.

Buy Plants, Bulbs, and Supplies

Although you can probably find all the plants and bulbs for this garden at your local garden center or nursery, it's fun to spend a dreary winter day paging through catalogs. See "Where to Buy" on the opposite page for some companies that offer a good selection of rock garden plants.

In addition to the plants and bulbs listed for this garden, you'll need the following supplies:

• Three 40-pound bags of compost or composted manure. Or substitute homemade compost—one full bin or three wheelbarrows full.

- Rocks of your choice to create the rockscape of your garden

- Gravel to improve soil drainage

- One 5-pound bag of natural organic fertilizer

- One large watering can

SEASON TWO (MARCH, APRIL, AND MAY)

Prepare the Site

The best way to have a successful rock garden is to build it from scratch. That way you can eliminate weeds that may compete with your plants and also provide the rock plants with the well-drained soil they relish. You can start building your rock garden any time the soil is warm and dry enough to be worked.

To prepare the site, work the soil as deep as you can, adding compost or composted manure to lighten it up and improve drainage. If your site doesn't already have excellent drainage, you may want to go the next step when preparing the soil: Dig the bed out to a depth of at least 2 feet, setting the soil on a tarp. Then add a 6-inch layer of very coarse gravel or large rocks on the bottom, and cover it with another 6-inch layer of medium- to large-size gravel.

WHERE TO BUY

Although there are mail-order companies specializing in rock garden plants, all of the plants in this garden are fairly common. You can buy them from your local garden center, or write to one of the following companies:

- Wayside Gardens, 1 Garden Lane, Hodges, SC 29695-0001

- White Flower Farm, P.O. Box 50, Litchfield, CT 06759-0050

Finally, top the site with an 8-inch layer of improved garden soil made by mixing your own garden soil or equivalent amounts of bagged topsoil with an equal amount of compost or composted manure.

If you already have a rocky area on your property that you would like to plant, you probably don't need to improve the drainage to this extent. But most expert rock gardeners would recommend replacing the soil between and around the rocks with a weed-free mix of compost and topsoil. It's a lot of work up front, but it will save you from weeding headaches in the long run.

Before you plant, thoroughly soak the soil until it seeps down into the gravel layer. Rock garden plants like the well-drained crevices between rocks that this soaking creates. It also helps to settle the garden soil.

Add the Rocks

Before we start talking about how to site your rocks for a natural-looking rock garden, let's discuss how to choose the right rocks. Pink quartz may be pretty, but it's going to look out of place in your garden. The best rocks for your garden are the ones that are found naturally in your yard or area. They'll look like they've been there forever, making your garden really believable. If you live in a rock-free area, try to decide what kind of rock you think would have been there

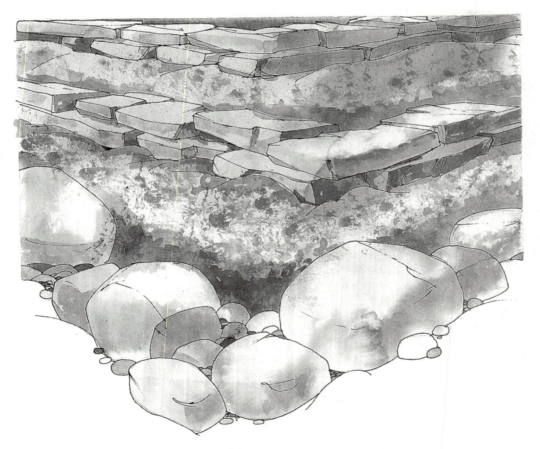

The style of rockwork you use will depend on the types of rocks you have to work with. Rocks that are native to your region will look most natural. Use a crowbar to position large rocks, if necessary.

For a natural-looking and stable rock garden, bury at least one-third of each of the larger rocks in your garden under the soil.

if there had been rocks. Then go for it.

Once you've chosen the rocks, you can start layering your surface stones in a horizontal pattern to create a terraced rock garden. First, place an irregular layer of stones around the perimeter of the garden to form a rim. You can make a solid wall all the way around or arrange a few larger rocks at various intervals. All of these stones need to be sunk into the soil a little bit for stability, but sink some in more than others and let some rise above the others to form little valleys and mountains. Try to create a natural effect so the rocks look like they've always been there. Avoid vertical drops

that will turn into raging gulleys during a rainstorm; gentle horizontal surfaces are your best bet.

Fill in some of the gaps between the stones with more of the topsoil and compost mixture. Place two more terraced bands of stone horizontally across the bed to form three distinct planting terraces. Fill in gaps with more improved soil mixture, and water the entire garden again to settle the new soil around the new stones.

Plant the Garden

Although all the plants in this garden are very hardy, it's best to wait until danger of frost is past to plant them. Try to time your planting for an overcast day, or at least wait until late in the afternoon so the plants will not be withered by the hot sun.

When you are ready to plant, bring all of your plants out to the garden site. For this garden, you'll have to use my design on page 250 as a general suggestion only. The rocks you've chosen for the garden and the way you've arranged them will determine where you plant. It's a good idea to arrange your plants at least in one section of the garden at a time, then step back and look at the arrangement before planting anything.

If you have followed my design, start at the left side of the garden and work down the bed—planting the miniature rose and basket-of-gold first and the violet sage and lavender at the far right side last. If you are adjusting the design to suit your own rock pattern, keep in mind that I've put the tallest plants—the blanket flower, catmint, cranesbill, flax, and lavender—near the center of the garden. Try to do the same in your own arrangement. Stair-step the medium-size and smaller plants as you move toward the front of the garden, so the very smallest are in front where they're easy to see. As you arrange your plants, be sure to leave spaces open for the daffodils and tulips you'll plant in the fall.

A narrow-bladed hand trowel is ideal for planting a rock garden. It allows you to really get into the small spaces between the rocks. To plant your rock garden, use your trowel to loosen the soil and dig a hole large enough to hold the root ball of your plant comfortably. It is very important that your plant's roots have plenty of room to spread out. Make the hole deep enough so that the crown of the plant (the point where the roots join the main stem) is planted at soil level. You may need to rearrange some of the stones in your rock garden to accommodate the root systems of your plants.

Rock garden plants don't demand a lot of extra fertilizer. Work slightly less than 1 tablespoon of balanced natural organic fertilizer into the soil as you loosen it to plant. After that, an annual application of the natural organic fertilizer will help the plants get the nourishment they need.

Place the plant in the hole, fill in with soil, and press down with your hands. Then gather soil around the stem and press down again to eliminate any air pockets. Water thoroughly.

SEASON THREE
(JUNE, JULY, AND AUGUST)

Minimize Chores and Enjoy Your Garden

I like to think of tending a rock garden as being really like tending my houseplants. Plants in a rock garden need a little extra care, but none of the work you do will be heavy or strenuous. Tending a rock garden can be beneficial for you as well as for your plants. It's relaxing, enjoyable work and a great way to unwind.

In the early summer, after the plants are growing well, sprinkle slightly less than 1 tablespoon of natural organic fertilizer around the base of each plant and work it into the soil lightly with your fingertips. This little bit of fertilizer will help the plant develop strong roots and pretty flowers.

This is one of the few gardens you will ever grow where a heavy layer of natural organic mulch is not recommended to control weeds and retain moisture. Because of the rather diminutive nature of the plants themselves and the rather small growing space each plant has, a thick bed of mulch might retard an adequate circulation of air around the plants and retain too much moisture near the soil surface. And if there's one thing rock garden plants don't appreciate, it's sitting with their roots and crowns in soil that is too moist. A heavy mulch might promote too much water retention when what you want is good drainage.

Instead, you are going to have to rely on hand weeding and judicious watering. As far as weeding is concerned, as long as the soil you have used to build your rock garden is relatively free of weed seeds, and you don't already have a rock garden that has been overrun with noxious weeds, a quick weeding once a week will be adequate. In fact, if you visit your garden frequently to see how your plants are doing, you'll probably pull a weed or two anyway. That may be all the weeding your garden needs.

Watering is essential for a rock garden. Because the soil needs to be very well drained, it can tend to dry out too much. In addition, there's so little soil in a rock garden that it tends to dry out faster than a larger conventional garden. I advise you to water your rock garden by hand with a watering can. Sprinkle the water gently around your plants until the ground is soaked. During the rainy weeks of the year, you probably won't have to water your rock garden at all. Once the rains have stopped and the weather begins to dry out, I suggest watering once a week. The best times are early morning before you go to work or early evening.

SEASON FOUR (SEPTEMBER AND OCTOBER)

Plant the Bulbs

Now is the time to buy and plant the daffodil and tulip bulbs. To plant, take the bulbs out to the garden and spread them out on the soil surface so they cover as much of their planting sites as possible. Don't crowd your bulbs; plant them no closer than 2 inches apart. If you have any bulbs left over, simply tuck them in somewhere on the edge of the garden where nothing else is growing.

Using a narrow-bladed trowel, if you have one, dig holes 6 to 8 inches deep for the daffodils and 4 to 6 inches deep for the tulips, and place a bulb in the bottom of each hole. Cover the holes with soil and press down firmly with your hands to make sure no air pockets remain around the bulbs.

Prepare the Garden for Winter

Your rock garden will need a layer of mulch to protect the plants from freeze-thaw cycles that can heave them out of the soil in winter. Wait until the weather has turned quite cold and the tops of the plants have died or gone into dormancy. Mulching while the weather is still warm can encourage the plants to send out new growth that would be damaged once the really cold weather arrives.

Once cold weather has finally arrived and the ground is frozen or as cold as it is going to get, cut any blackened, dead growth off the tops of the plants. Then cover the whole garden with salt hay—grasses cut in salt marshes along the Atlantic coast—or choose straw or shredded or composted leaves. You can even use branches that have been cut from ever-green trees (your Christmas tree is ideal for this—just cut the branches off and lay them over the garden). Don't use regular hay because it is apt to be full of weed seeds. You can use whole leaves, but they can mat down when wet and cause rot. If you do decide to use whole leaves, use oak leaves, which mat down the least; avoid maple leaves, which mat down like crazy.

Next spring, don't be in too much of a hurry to remove the protective covering. Rock gardens are more sensitive to temperature changes than ordinary gardens. As the weather begins to warm up, look under the protective covering to see if any new green shoots are sprouting up. If they are, remove the mulch gradually (and carefully!) until the plant is growing well. These plants are very hardy and a little spring frost won't hurt them, but there is no sense in exposing them to a sudden cold snap when it isn't necessary.

After you've removed the covering, you might notice that some of the plants have been pushed up out of the ground a little. Carefully press them back down in their spots and add a little bit of compost or improved topsoil around the plants.

Now that you know the basics, your rock garden will bring you years of low-maintenance pleasure.

Don't Get Bogged Down

Turn a Soggy Site
into a Beautiful Garden

A WET, SOGGY SITE CAN BE A NIGHTMARE *when you're trying to grow a lawn on it. If you can mow it at all, the mower bogs down in the mud; if not, it's a weedy eyesore. But a wet site in full sun is the perfect place for some of the prettiest flowers and lushest greenery you've ever seen.*

Swamp azalea lights up the garden with pink flowers in spring; the red berries of winterberry glow from fall into winter. Large perennials, including bigleaf ligularia, goat's beard, rodgersia, and ferns, add a bold, almost tropical-looking touch to the garden. Add easy-care perennials with beautiful flowers and you have a stunning garden. Just don't tell anyone how much work it saves you!

10′ × 20′

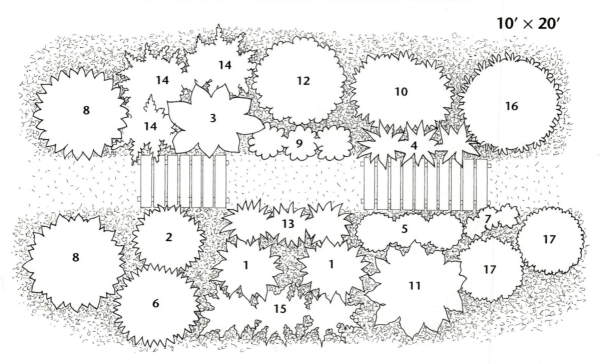

1. Astilbe
2. Bee balm
3. Bigleaf ligularia
4. Blue flag irises
5. Cardinal flowers
6. Goat's beard
7. Japanese primroses
8. Joe-Pye weed
9. Marsh marigolds
10. Pink turtlehead
11. Rodgersia
12. Rose mallow
13. Yellow flags
14. Ostrich ferns
15. Royal ferns
16. Swamp azalea
17. Winterberries

SHRUBS TO BUY

- Swamp azalea. Buy one.
- Winterberries. Buy one male and one female.

FERNS TO BUY

Buy three of each of the following ferns:

- Ostrich ferns
- Royal ferns

Turn an eyesore into a beautiful garden when you replace struggling lawn grass with these beautiful ferns and flowers.

PLANTS TO BUY

Buy one of each of the following perennials, unless otherwise noted:

- Astilbe. Buy two.
- Bee balm
- Bigleaf ligularia
- Blue flag irises. Buy three.
- Cardinal flowers. Buy two or three.
- Goat's beard
- Japanese primroses. Buy three.
- Joe-Pye weed
- Marsh marigolds. Buy two or three.
- Pink turtlehead
- Rodgersia
- Rose mallow
- Yellow flags. Buy three.

THE PLANT GUIDE

PLANTS FOR A BOGGY GARDEN

ALL OF THE PLANTS in this garden like wet feet. They'll all thrive in soil that's not just damp—it's downright wet. In fact, many of them, including bigleaf ligularia, goat's beard, and rodgersia, need soil that stays constantly moist to grow well. The yellow and blue flags will grow in 1 or 2 inches of standing water as well as on well-drained sites.

Plants

Buy one plant of each of the following moisture-loving perennials, unless otherwise noted:

Astilbes (*Astilbe* spp.). There are a dozen or more species and cultivars of astilbe commonly offered in garden centers and nurseries. Heights range from 1 to 3 feet, and the big, airy flower heads appear from June through August, de-pending on the type you buy. For this garden, I suggest you choose plants that are about 2 feet tall and have either white or pink flowers. Buy two plants. Zones 3 to 9.

Bee balm (*Monarda didyma*). Also known as Oswego tea, bee balm is a bushy 2- to 4-foot plant with pungent, minty leaves. It bears moplike heads of red, pink, or white flowers for most of the summer. For this garden, I suggest a pink- or white-flowered cultivar, such as 'Croftway Pink', 'Marshall's Delight' (both pink), or 'Snow White'. Plants will spread. Zones 4 to 8.

Bigleaf ligularia (*Ligularia dentata*). The bold, tropical-looking 20-inch leaves of this perennial are purplish green above and deep reddish purple below. Plants grow in clumps 3 to 4 feet tall and are topped by clusters of bright, daisylike, yellow-orange flowers in late summer. Zones 3 to 8.

Blue flag iris (*Iris versicolor*). This native American iris loves moist soil and grows along streams and pond edges. Plants produce pale violet-blue flowers on 2- to 3-foot stems in late spring or early summer and have attractive strap-shaped leaves. Buy three plants to establish a clump. Zones 2 to 8.

Cardinal flower (*Lobelia cardinalis*). These water-loving plants grow on the edges of streams and ponds—anywhere the soil is moist. Plants range from 2 to 4 feet tall, and the top third of the spike is covered with flaming red flowers, which both butterflies and hummingbirds adore. Great blue lobelia (*L. siphilitica*), cardinal flower's cousin, is a good alternative, or use them together to make a stunning combination. Buy two or three plants to establish a colony. Plants will spread. Zones 2 to 9.

Goat's beard (*Aruncus dioicus*). This shrub-size perennial grows 3 to 6 feet tall and equally wide. Foot-long plumes of small white flowers appear in June or July. Zones 3 to 7.

Japanese primrose (*Primula japonica*). Also known as candelabra primrose, this lovely wetland dweller sends up nearly 2-foot stems topped with pink, red, or white flowers in late spring and early summer. Buy three plants to start a colony; they

self-sow. Zones 5 to 8.

Joe-Pye weed (*Eupatorium purpureum*). I think, hands down, that Joe-Pye weed is the glory of the bog garden. Plants range from 3 to 6 feet tall, depending on how much moisture they get, and they spread like crazy. The light purple or pale rose flowers appear in late summer and early fall. Buy one plant and divide it in a year to form the second clump shown on the design on page 264, or buy two plants right from the start. Zones 3 to 8.

Marsh marigold (*Caltha palustris*). Marsh marigold bears bright yellow flowers and glossy, heart-shaped leaves on an 8- to 20-inch plant. Plants bloom from April until June then disappear after flowering. Buy two or three plants to form a cluster. Zones 2 to 8.

Pink turtlehead (*Chelone lyonii*). Dark green foliage sets off the pink flowers of this vigorous wildling quite nicely. Flowers, each shaped like a turtle's head with its mouth open, appear in late summer and early fall on 1- to 3-foot plants. Zones 3 to 8.

Rodgersias (*Rodgersia* spp.). Choose either fingerleaf rodgersia (*R. aesculifolia*) or bronze rodgersia (*R. podophylla*) for this garden. Both are large-leaved plants with crinkled foliage that flowers in early summer.

Fingerleaf rodgersia grows 4 to 6 feet tall, bears 2-foot clusters of white flowers, and is hardy in Zones 4 to 7. Bronze-leaf rodgersia reaches 5 feet tall, has coppery-colored leaves and clusters of yellowish white flowers. It is hardy in Zones 5 to 7.

Rose mallow (*Hibiscus moscheutos*). This shrub-size American native is as gaudy as any flower plant breeders have ever dreamed up. Plants range from 4 to 8 feet tall and are covered from summer until fall with pink, 17-inch flowers. It's been described as "a hollyhock on steroids." A popular cultivar is 'Disco Belle'. Zones 5 to 10; to Zone 4, if you protect the plants with evergreen boughs in winter.

Yellow flag (*Iris pseudacorus*). Like blue flag iris, this native iris is at home anywhere the soil is damp—along streams and pond edges or in low spots where water settles. It produces clumps of strap-shaped foliage that are attractive all summer. The lovely yellow flowers appear on 2-foot stems in spring. Buy three plants. Zones 5 to 9.

Ferns

To start colonies of each of these native American ferns, buy three plants of each. Both spread by underground runners.

Ostrich fern (*Matteuccia pensylvanica*). Dark green, plumelike

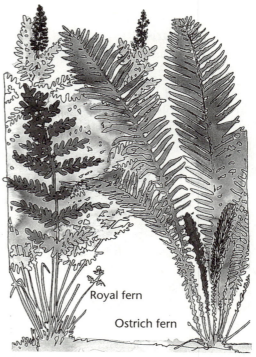

Royal fern

Ostrich fern

Your soil's moisture content will determine how large your ferns grow. The more moisture, the larger the fronds.

fronds can reach 5 feet tall in spots where the plants get plenty of water. Zones 2 to 8.

Royal fern (*Osmunda regalis*). Large, broad-leaved fronds give this fern a tropical look. The plants can reach 5 to 6 feet, if they are growing in moist to damp soil. Zones 3 to 9.

Shrubs

Anyone who has tried to keep a shrub alive in a damp site knows that it's often a lost cause. Some shrubs, though, positively love having wet roots. The two shrubs I've chosen for this design, swamp azalea and winterberry holly, are especially good for a boggy area. Besides growing well, they each have a special bonus—fragrant flowers in the case of the azalea and, for the holly, bright red berries that birds love. Plant them and see for yourself!

Swamp azalea (*Rhododendron viscosum*). Clove-scented white to pale pink flowers appear in June or early July on this native flowering shrub. Plants are deciduous and generally grow 6 to 8 feet tall. Buy one plant. Zones 3 to 9.

Winterberry (*Ilex verticillata*). Winterberry is a deciduous holly that produces small white flowers in spring, green leaves all summer long, and fabulous red berries that last well into winter. Because this holly loses its leaves in fall, the berries really stand out. Plants range from 6 to 10 feet tall. In order to get fruit, you'll need to buy one male and one or more females for pollination. Several improved cultivars are worth looking for because they hold their berries longer into winter than the original species. Ask for 'Sparkleberry' or 'Winter Red'; both are female cultivars. 'Apollo' is a good male cultivar. Zones 3 to 9.

THE SEASONAL GUIDE

SEASON ONE (JANUARY AND FEBRUARY)

Select a Site

Choosing a site is really the only hurdle you have to overcome to plant this garden. Since this garden features a variety of vigorous plants, once you've found a site that provides the damp soil they love, they'll do nearly all the rest of the work for you. And if you have a boggy or damp site, you don't need me to tell you where to place this garden. You already know because you've been trying to figure out what to do with it for as long as you've owned your property.

All the plants in this garden grow best in full sun—at least six hours of direct sunlight each day. However, almost of them will tolerate a little shade, although they'll grow a little slower and bloom a little less.

Buy Plants and Supplies

Most of the plants in this garden can be grown from seed, but I recommend that you buy plants instead. You'll get bigger plants faster, and most are readily available from garden centers and nurseries. Or send for catalogs now so you can order plants in plenty of time for spring planting. See "Where to Buy" on this page for a list of sources.

In addition to the plants listed for this garden, you'll need the following supplies:

• Two 40-pound bags of compost or composted manure. Or substitute homemade compost—one full bin or three wheelbarrows full.

• One 2½-pound bag of natural organic fertilizer

• Six large bags of shredded organic mulch, such as pine bark,

WHERE TO BUY

You may need to order from more than one company to find all the plants for this garden. Here's a list of catalogs that carry many of the plants listed for this design:

• André Viette Farm and Nursery, Route 1, Box 16, Fishersville, VA 22939

• Holbrook Farm & Nursery, 115 Lance Road, P.O. Box 368, Fletcher, NC 28732

• Roslyn Nursery, 211 Burrs Lane, Dix Hills, NY 11746

• Wayside Gardens, 1 Garden Lane, Hodges, SC 29695-0001

• White Flower Farm, P.O. Box 50, Litchfield, CT 06759-0050.

cedar bark, or pine needles. Or substitute an equivalent amount of your own compost or a mix of compost and shredded leaves.

• Two 4-cubic-foot bags of more organic matter such as compost, chopped leaves, or rotted sawdust

SEASON TWO
(MARCH, APRIL, AND MAY)

Prepare the Site

This is not a garden where you are going to go out and till up an area with a rotary tiller, unless you happen to begin preparing the soil during the summer months when even the boggiest areas tend to dry out a little bit. Damp soil will just cling to the tines of the tiller and gum up the works. Instead, you'll need to do all of the digging by hand, adding organic matter to the soil as you go, and then covering the area with a lot of mulch to keep weeds down.

Start your garden by clearing away weeds and other debris and digging out as much grass and as many weed roots as possible. Anything growing there now is right at home in wet soil. It will come back to haunt you unless you dig it out roots and all. Leave any large rocks or tree stumps, though. They will give the garden interesting contours or texture.

Plant the Garden

Since you are working with a wet garden site, you can plant this garden in either the late spring or early summer. Just be sure to let the soil dry out enough for you to dig in it. (See "Getting Your Garden Ready to Plant" on page 42 for complete information on preparing the soil.) If your site floods in spring, be sure to wait until all danger of flooding is past.

The plan for this garden covers a boggy area that's about 10 feet by 20

feet. There's a mulched path down the center so you can enjoy your flowers up close. You can add a simple plank bridge, as shown on page 273, if your site gets really wet. Or just mulch your path deeply and don't wear your good shoes into the garden. If you have a larger area, by all means buy more plants and simply plant larger clumps with the same general plan. If you have a stream to plant, you can plant half of the garden on either side of it.

When you're ready to plant, gather up all your plants and take them out to the garden. Arrange them in the spots where you want to plant them, either using the garden design on page 264 or your own design. Then, before you plant anything, step back and look at the garden from several angles to see if you like the arrangement.

To follow my design, place the Joe-Pye weed first. Choose a spot on the north or west side of the area so it won't block the sun for the rest of the garden. Place the swamp azalea and winterberries next—on the outer edges of your area.

Place the bigleaf ligularia, ferns, goat's beard, rodgersia, and rose mallow next. They take up spots in the back and middle part of the garden because they can grow up to 5 feet tall. Then place the astilbes, bee balm, cardinal flowers, and pink turtlehead between the taller plants. Fill in the rest of the garden with the remaining plants, putting the smaller flags, marsh marigolds, and primroses along the path in the center so they aren't hidden by the taller plants.

Except for the yellow and blue flag irises, all of the plants in this garden are planted in the same way. Dig a hole large enough to accommodate the roots of the plant comfortably—be sure to give them plenty of room. Work a shovelful or trowelful of compost and a handful of natural organic fertilizer into the soil in the hole. Remove the plant from its container and place it in the hole so that the crown of the plant (where the roots join the main body of the plant) is at ground level. Fill the hole with soil and gather additional soil around the plant and press down firmly with your hands. Water each plant thoroughly.

For the flag irises, which have somewhat longer roots, dig the hole a little larger and deeper than those for the rest of the plants. Work a little organic matter and natural organic fertilizer into the soil in the hole. Then place the plant in the hole so the roots have room to stretch out and barely cover them with soil. Press down firmly and water thoroughly.

Finish planting by spreading mulch over the entire garden to control weeds. Keep the mulch 1 inch away from all the perennials and 2 inches away from the trunks of the shrubs.

SEASON THREE
(JUNE, JULY, AND AUGUST)

Minimize Chores and Enjoy Your Garden

To be sure your transplants get off to a good start, water them thoroughly once a week for the first month or two. After that, since the site you selected for this garden is boggy to begin with, you shouldn't have to water the garden during the rest of the year.

If this area gets flooded with moving water, your biggest chore will be to replenish the mulch that's protecting the soil and keeping down weeds. If it is only slightly flooded with calm water, you will still have to add more mulch, but not as much. But if all you have to do to maintain a beautiful garden each year is add a little mulch, that's not too bad.

Throughout the season, add more mulch or compost if any weeds pop up. Once you have smothered them long enough, they will eventually die and not bother you anymore. For

MAKE THIS SIMPLE BOG-GARDEN BRIDGE

You don't have to be an expert carpenter to make a bridge that will cover the wettest part of your path. To build one, you need two rough decay-resistant planks—either 2 × 10 or 2 × 12 planks are fine. (Rough planks made from cedar work best because cedar is decay-resistant, and the rough surface prevents slipping.) Nail the planks side by side onto short lengths of decay-resistant 2 × 4s.

Space the 2 × 4s about 48 inches apart, and secure them to the planks by nailing three 16d nails into each plank.

Then all you need to do is put your bridge over the wettest part of your path. If you need a longer bridge, butt two or three plank walkways end to end. If the ground is not exactly flat or the path turns, make shorter walkways.

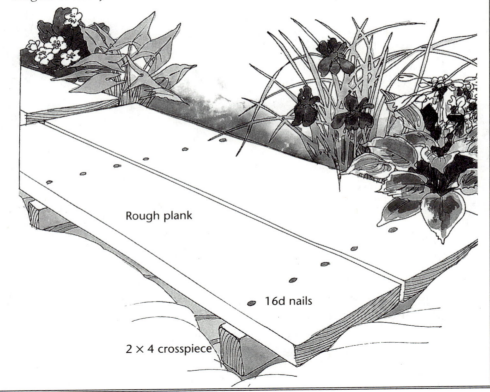

Rough plank

16d nails

2 × 4 crosspiece

persistent weeds, try adding a section of newspaper or two and then cover it with an additional layer of mulch.

You don't need to do too much else except enjoy this garden. Be sure to cut off any dead or spent flowers to encourage new growth. You can also make a fine bouquet from the bee balm, cardinal flowers, goat's beard, rodgersia, and rose mallow, which bloom at the same time. Joe-Pye weed also makes a great bouquet in the fall; so does pink turtlehead. Don't be alarmed if these flowers just bloom a little the first year. Once they've settled in, they will produce plenty of flowers next year.

SEASON FOUR (SEPTEMBER AND OCTOBER)

Prepare the Garden for Winter

As the colder weather arrives and the plants begin to die back from frost, cut them down to within 1 to 2 inches of the ground. Break up these cuttings and other plant debris and place it in your compost bin. Leave the azalea and winterberries alone. You won't need to prune them for many years.

Once the cold weather arrives and the season is over, place a light layer

of mulch or shredded leaves over the garden to protect it from the winter cold and to add extra organic matter to the soil.

The bee balm, cardinal flowers, ferns, Joe-Pye weed, and pink turtlehead will spread by themselves over the years to fill in your bog site quite naturally. Every three years or so, you can dig up clumps of these plants in the fall and give them away to friends.

Main clump

Offset

You don't have to dig the entire clump of either ostrich or royal fern to share a division with a friend. Slip your shovel between the main clump and one of the many small ferns, called offsets, around the base of the clump. Just dig out the offset, leaving the clump in place.

USDA Plant Hardiness Zone Map

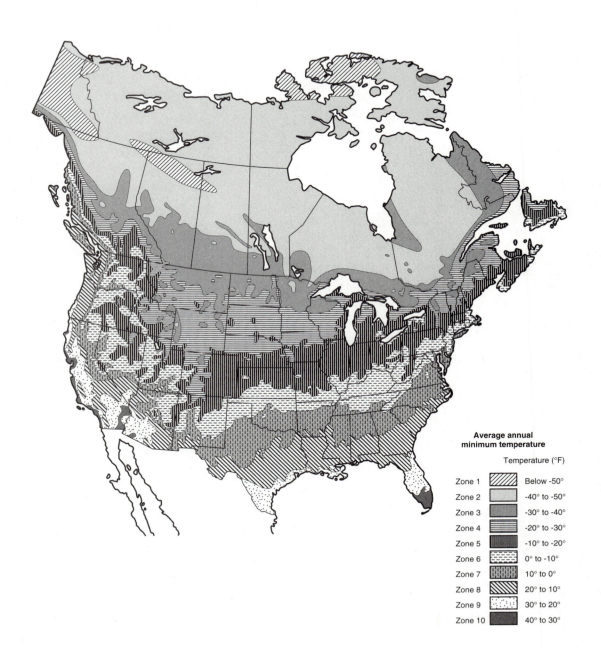

**Average annual
minimum temperature**

Temperature (°F)

Zone		Temperature
Zone 1		Below -50°
Zone 2		-40° to -50°
Zone 3		-30° to -40°
Zone 4		-20° to -30°
Zone 5		-10° to -20°
Zone 6		0° to -10°
Zone 7		10° to 0°
Zone 8		20° to 10°
Zone 9		30° to 20°
Zone 10		40° to 30°

Resources

The following mail-order companies are listed according to the types of plants or garden supplies they offer. For best results, buy plants that have been grown in the region of the country where you live.

Annuals, Bulbs, and Perennials

André Viette Farm & Nursery
Route 1, Box 16
Fishersville, VA 22939

Bluestone Perennials
7211 Middle Ridge Road
Madison, OH 44057

Carroll Gardens
P.O. Box 310
Westminster, MD 21158

The Daffodil Mart
Route 3, Box 794
Gloucester, VA 23061

Dutch Gardens
P.O. Box 200
Adelphia, NJ 07710

Ed Hume Seeds, Inc.
P.O. Box 1450
Kent, WA 98035

Gurney's Seed & Nursery Co.
110 Capital Street
Yankton, SD 57079

Henry Field's Seed & Nursery Co.
415 North Burnett
Shenandoah, IA 51602

Holbrook Farm & Nursery
115 Lance Road
P.O. Box 368
Fletcher, NC 28732

Jackson & Perkins Co.
1 Rose Lane
Medford, OR 97501

Klehm Nursery
4210 N. Duncan Road
Champaign, IL 61821

Kurt Bluemel, Inc.
2740 Greene Lane
Baldwin, MD 21013

Milaeger's Gardens
4838 Douglas Avenue
Racine, WI 53402-2498

Park Seed Co.
Cokesbury Road
Greenwood, SC 29647

Roses of Yesterday & Today
802 Brown's Valley Road
Watsonville, CA 95076

Roslyn Nursery
211 Burrs Lane
Dix Hills, NY 11746

Seeds of Change
P.O. Box 15700
Santa Fe, NM 87506

Shepherd's Garden Seeds
30 Irene Street
Torrington, CT 06790

Spring Hill Nurseries
6523 North Galena Road
Peoria, IL 61656

Stokes Seeds, Inc.
P.O. Box 548
Buffalo, NY 14240-0548

Thompson & Morgan, Inc.
P.O. Box 1308
Jackson, NJ 08527

Van Bourgondien Bros., Inc.
P.O. Box 1000
245 Farmingdale Road
Babylon, NY 11702

W. Atlee Burpee & Co.
300 Park Avenue
Warminster, PA 18974

Wayside Gardens
1 Garden Lane
Hodges, SC 29695-0001

White Flower Farm
P.O. Box 50
Litchfield, CT 06759-0050

Wildflowers and Native Plants

Applewood Seed Co.
5380 Vivian Street
Arvada, CO 80002

Niche Gardens
1111 Dawson Road
Chapel Hill, NC 27516

Plants of the Southwest
Route 6, Box 11-A
Sante Fe, NM 87501

Prairie Nursery
West 5859 Dyke Avenue
P.O. Box 306
Westfield, WI 53964

We-Du Nurseries
Route 5, Box 724
Marion, NC 28752

Tools, Supplies, and Garden Accessories

Gardener's Supply Co.
128 Intervale Road
Burlington, VT 05401-2850

Gardens Alive!
5100 Schenley Place
Lawrenceburg, IN 47025

Kinsman Company, Inc.
River Road
Point Pleasant, PA 18950

Peaceful Valley Farm Supply
P.O. Box 2209
Grass Valley, CA 95945

Smith & Hawken
25 Corte Madera
Mill Valley, CA 94941

Recommended Reading

Flower Gardening

Benjamin, Joan, and Barbara W. Ellis, eds. *Rodale's No-Fail Flower Garden*. Emmaus, Pa.: Rodale Press, 1994.

Harper, Pamela, and Frederick McGourty. *Perennials: How to Select, Grow, and Enjoy*. Los Angeles: Price Stern Sloan, 1985.

McClure, Susan, and C. Colston Burrell. *Rodale's Successful Organic Gardening: Perennials*. Emmaus, Pa.: Rodale Press, 1993.

Michalak, Patricia S. *Rodale's Successful Organic Gardening: Herbs*. Emmaus, Pa.: Rodale Press, 1993.

Oster, Maggie. *The Rose Book: How to Grow Roses Organically and Use Them in Over 50 Beautiful Crafts*. Emmaus, Pa.: Rodale Press, 1994.

Phillips, Ellen, and C. Colston Burrell. *Rodale's Illustrated Encyclopedia of Perennials*. Emmaus, Pa.: Rodale Press, 1993.

Schenk, George. *The Complete Shade Gardener*. Boston: Houghton Mifflin Co., 1991.

Smith, Marny, with Nancy DuBrule. *A Country Garden for Your Backyard*. Emmaus, Pa.: Rodale Press, 1992.

Taylor, Norman. *Taylor's Guide to Annuals*. Rev. ed. Boston: Houghton Mifflin Co., 1986.

———. *Taylor's Guide to Bulbs*. Rev. ed. Boston: Houghton Mifflin Co., 1986.

Wildflowers

Art, Henry W. *The Wildflower Gardener's Guide: Northeast, Mid-Atlantic, Great Lakes, and Eastern Canada Edition*. Pownal, Vt.: Storey Communications, Garden Way Publishing, 1987.

Phillips, Harry R. *Growing and Propagating Wildflowers*. Edited by J. Kenneth Moore and C. Ritchie Bell. Chapel Hill, N.C.: University of North Carolina Press, 1985.

General Gardening

Bradley, Fern Marshall, and Barbara W. Ellis, eds. *Rodale's All-New Encyclopedia of Organic Gardening*. Emmaus, Pa.: Rodale Press, 1992.

Brooklyn Botanic Garden. *American Gardens: A Traveler's Guide*. Brooklyn, N.Y.: Brooklyn Botanic Garden, 1986.

Dirr, Michael A. *Manual of Woody Landscape Plants*. 4th ed. Champaign, Ill.: Stipes Publishing Co., 1990.

Ellis, Barbara W., ed. *Rodale's Illustrated Encyclopedia of Gardening and Landscaping Techniques*. Emmaus, Pa.: Rodale Press, 1990.

Ellis, Barbara W., Joan Benjamin, and Deborah L. Martin. *Rodale's Low Maintenance Gardening Techniques*. Emmaus, Pa.: Rodale Press, 1995.

Hynes, Erin. *Rodale's Successful Organic Gardening: Improving the Soil*. Emmaus, Pa.: Rodale Press, 1994.

Rosenfeld, Lois G., ed. *The Garden Tourist*. New York: The Garden Tourist Press, 1995.

Roth, Susan A. *The Four-Season Landscape*. Emmaus, Pa.: Rodale Press, 1994.

Sombke, Laurence. *Beautiful Easy Gardens*. Old Saybrook, Ct.: The Globe Pequot Press, 1993.

———. "The Natural Gardener" newsletter. Contact Laurence Sombke, P.O. Box 36, Hollowville, NY 12536.

Taylor's Guide Staff. *Taylor's Guide to Shrubs*. Boston: Houghton Mifflin Co., 1987

———. *Taylor's Guide to Trees*. Boston: Houghton Mifflin Co., 1988

Organic Pest and Disease Control

Carr, Anna. *Rodale's Color Handbook of Garden Insects*. Emmaus, Pa.: Rodale Press, 1979.

Michalak, Patricia S., and Linda A. Gilkeson. *Rodale's Successful Organic Gardening: Controlling Pests and Diseases*. Emmaus, Pa.: Rodale Press, 1994.

Smith, Miranda, and Anna Carr. *Rodale's Garden Insect, Disease and Weed Identification Guide*. Emmaus, Pa.: Rodale Press, 1988.

Birds, Butterflies, and Wildlife

Proctor, Noble. *Garden Birds*. Emmaus, Pa.: Rodale Press, 1986.

———. *Songbirds: How to Attract Them and Identify Their Songs*. Emmaus, Pa.: Rodale Press, 1988.

Schneck, Marcus. *Butterflies: How to Identify and Attract Them to Your Garden*. Emmaus, Pa.: Rodale Press, 1990.

———. *Your Backyard Wildlife Garden*. Emmaus, Pa.: Rodale Press, 1992.

Index

Note: Page references in **boldface** indicate illustrations. *Italic* references indicate photographs.